# THE CAPITAL RING

D0514496

Also available:
*The Cotswold Way*
*The Dales Way*
*The Saxon Shore Way*
*The West Highland Way*
*The Two Moors Way*
*The Southern Upland Way*
*The Heart of England Way*
*The Wye Valley Walk*
*The Cumbria Way*
*The Wessex Ridgeway*
*The London Loop*

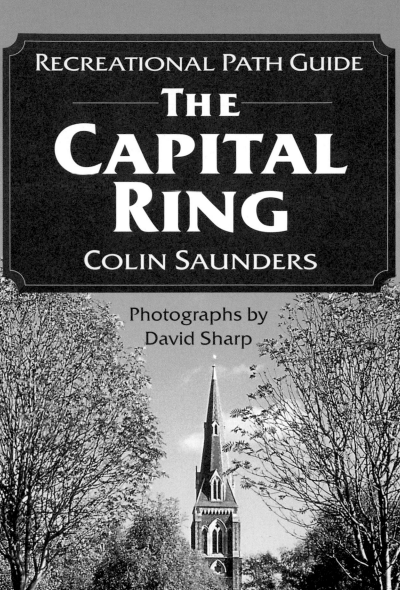

RECREATIONAL PATH GUIDE

# THE
# CAPITAL
# RING

## COLIN SAUNDERS

Photographs by
David Sharp

Aurum Press

# Acknowledgements

The Capital Ring owes its existence to the imagination and hard work of many people. The idea was Roger Warhurst's, and Brian Bellwood led a team of researchers who walked out the proposed route. Jim Walker, Stuart McLeod and the Orbitals Working Party of the London Walking Forum co-ordinated discussions with the London boroughs, and an army of officers from the London boroughs helped with finalising the route and providing details for this book. Many other individuals and organisations have contributed snippets of information. Last, but certainly not least, the author is especially grateful to David Sharp, chairman of the Orbitals Working Party, for providing the photographs and checking the route description.

First published 2003 by Aurum Press Limited
25 Bedford Avenue, London WC1B 3AT

Text copyright © Colin Saunders 2003
Photographs copyright © David Sharp 2003

**Ordnance Survey** This product includes mapping data licensed from Ordnance Survey® with the permission of the Controller of Her Majesty's Stationery Office. © Crown copyright 2003. All rights reserved. Licence number 43453U.

Ordnance Survey and Travelmaster are registered trademarks and the Ordnance Survey symbol and Explorer trademarks of Ordnance Survey, the national mapping agency of Great Britain.

A catalogue record for this book is available from the British Library.

ISBN 1 85410 894 8

1 3 5 7 9 10 8 6 4 2
2003 2005 2007 2006 2004

Book design by Robert Updegraff
Printed and bound in Italy by Printer Trento Srl

Cover photograph: *Maryon Wilson Park, Charlton (Walk 1)*
Title-page photograph: *St Mary's, Hanwell, from Brent Lodge Park (Walk 8)*

# Contents

# Distance checklist

# HOW TO USE THIS GUIDE

The format of this book is similar to that of its companion, *The London Loop* by David Sharp, also published by Aurum Press. The introduction sets out background and general information, which should set the scene and help you understand how the route was conceived and planned. It tells you something about the London Walking Forum, without which the route would never have got up and running. It goes on to describe the route in general, the signs, and the plentiful public transport opportunities. There is some advice on walking safely, and on how accessible the route is for people using wheelchairs and buggies. Finally, the introduction puts in perspective the historical background to the area covered by the Capital Ring.

Next, the Capital Ring is described in detail, divided into the 15 consecutive walks that have been planned jointly by the London Walking Forum and relevant London boroughs. On each walk there are official Capital Ring links with nearby stations, and these too are described. The route is marked on maps prepared specially by the Ordnance Survey® from their 1:25,000 Explorer™ maps, enlarged to 1:16,666 to show the route more clearly. With text and maps on facing pages, you should find it easy to follow the Capital Ring, whether the section you are on has been signed and waymarked or not. Letters are used to identify key points along the route, both in the text and on the maps. Special features of interest are numbered in the same way. Pubs, cafés, toilets, museums and car parks on or very near the route are identified by their individual logos on the maps. The total distances for each walk and the station links are shown to the nearest decimal point in miles and kilometres, elsewhere in miles and yards only. Station links and other diversions are shown in italics, to distinguish them from the main route description.

The final section contains more information about public transport, useful addresses, including the borough councils that are responsible for installation and maintenance of the signs and waymarks, and a list of the Ordnance Survey® maps that cover the route.

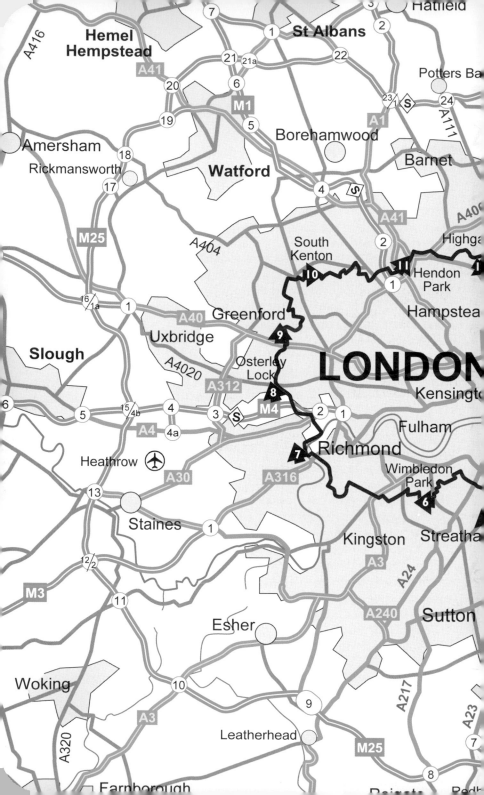

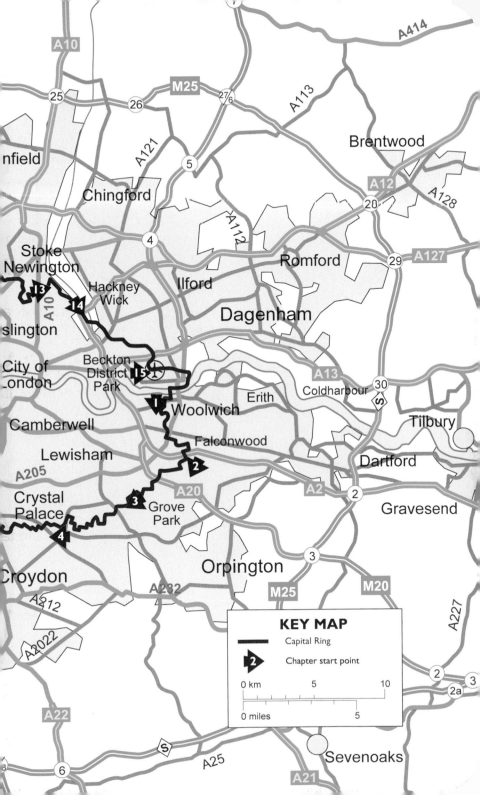

.

# Introduction

*Near the derelict chapel, Dr Isaac Watts gazes across Abney Park Cemetery in Stoke Newington, now a nature reserve (Walk 12).*

Approaching London from the air, passengers lucky enough to have window seats are often struck by the abundance of greenery that separates the suburbs and permeates the urban sprawl. Those green spaces may not be so easily found on the ground, but this book will guide you through at least 50 of them along the Capital Ring, a walking route of 75 miles (120 km) that is easily divided into bite-sized chunks. The green spaces are linked by stretches beside water and along pleasant residential roads, and you will pass many points of interest on the way.

The Capital Ring forms an inner circle for walkers around Greater London, while its big brother, the 150-mile London Loop, provides the outer circle. The Ring lies between 4 and 10 miles (6.4 and 16 km) from Charing Cross, on average about three-quarters of the way from central London to the Greater London boundary, while the Loop closely follows the boundary itself. In Travelcard terms, the Capital Ring meanders mostly through Zones 3 and 4, occasionally straying into Zone 2.

You will see some of London's outstanding attractions, such as the Thames Barrier, Eltham Palace, and Wimbledon Common with its windmill. And you pass by or through many nature reserves, including Richmond Park, where you can spot herds of deer, while Syon Park is virtually a theme park. There is waterside walking aplenty on the Thames and its tributaries, the Grand Union Canal, Brent Reservoir (Welsh Harp), the Lee Navigation and in Docklands. Green areas of all sizes along the route include parks, woods and even occasional farmland. You will come across some little-known gems, such as Oxleas Meadows, the Parkland Walk, Abney Park Cemetery, The Greenway and the Docklands Campus of the University of East London.

There are breathtaking views right from the start at Woolwich, where a vista along the River Thames includes the Thames Barrier, Canary Wharf and the Millennium Dome. From sea level at the outset, the route rises to several comparatively high points in London terms, reaching altitudes of around 300—400 feet (90—120 metres) with extensive panoramas. The Thames is a dominant feature of the route, encountered three times. Although it is nearly a quarter of a mile (half a kilometre) wide at Woolwich, this does not prevent you from completing the circle on foot, as it is possible to cross underwater through a foot tunnel.

## THE LONDON WALKING FORUM

The Capital Ring and the London Loop both encircle Greater London, linking many shorter routes in two extensive networks of trails. The proposal for these ambitious routes was first put forward in 1990 at one of the first meetings of the London Walking Forum. Coincidentally, a similar idea was being investigated by Bob Gilbert, whose book *The Green London Way*, published in 1991, describes a similar but longer route of 92 miles (147 km) around inner London. The Capital Ring differs further in that it is formally recognised by the Greater London Authority and London boroughs, and the route is on the way to being fully signed and waymarked.

The London Walking Forum was established in 1990 by representatives of the Countryside Commission (now the Countryside Agency), the Ramblers' Association, the London boroughs and others with an interest in walking. Many of the Forum's activities are now facilitated by Transport for London (TfL), an agency of the Greater London Authority. It co-ordinates the development of a multitude of trails that explore most of the capital's green areas and waterways. In this book, the other trails encountered along the Capital Ring are mentioned, and you can obtain details of them all from TfL Street Management's Walking Promotions Office, or in *London – the definitive walking guide*, by the same author (Cicerone Press, ISBN 1 85284 339 X).

## WALKING THE CAPITAL RING

The Capital Ring is divided into 15 separate walks, ranging from 3.3 to 8.2 miles (5.4 to 13.2 km) and averaging just under 5 miles (8 km). If you wish to cover the whole route, the logical starting place is of course the very beginning of Walk 1, on the south side of the Woolwich Foot Tunnel. But there is no compulsion to follow the sections in progressive order; you can join and leave at any convenient point in any order. In this book, the route is described clockwise, and it should therefore be easier to go in this direction, especially as the route was not fully signed at the time of writing. When signage is complete (scheduled for the end of 2003), it should be possible to follow the route in either direction as preferred. If you are walking in the early morning or late evening, or on Christmas Day, bear in mind that some of the smaller parks along the route may be closed — times can be checked with the parks department of the relevant London borough (see Useful Addresses, page 165).

*The magnificently carved front door of Charlton House, one of the best examples of a Jacobean building in London (Walk 1).*

*A typical Capital Ring aluminium street sign, showing the walking-man symbol and the Big Ben logo.*

# SIGNS AND WAYMARKS

A variety of signs and waymarks indicate the route on the ground. In open spaces these consist mostly of a simple white disc, mounted on wooden posts and containing a directional arrow with the Big Ben logo in blue and text in green — but note that in the London Boroughs of Kingston and Richmond black replaces green due to local conservation area considerations. A word of warning: the arrow's direction may not be clear until you are close up. It is easy to assume that it points ahead, but it may indicate a turn — look closely before continuing.

On streets, the posts are replaced by larger aluminium signs strapped to lampposts and other street furniture, and these additionally carry a walking-man symbol. At major focal points you will also encounter tall green-and-white signposts that give distances to three points in either direction. Some of these locations may also have information boards. It is intended that the link routes with stations will all be signed eventually, and on these the word 'link' is incorporated into the Capital Ring logo.

It is possible that some signs or waymarks may have been affected or removed by vandalism or accidental damage. When in doubt, it will probably be best to stick to the route description in this book. If you come across such instances, it would be appreciated if you could report them to the highways department of the relevant London borough (see Useful Addresses, page 165).

# REACHING THE CAPITAL RING

The route is designed to pass by or close to stations, and walkers should find using public transport most convenient. In fact, the route passes or has links to 45 stations, and there are many bus routes in between. Most lie within Travelcard Zones 2, 3 and 4 — just one (Harrow-on-the-Hill) is in Zone 5. For further details, see the Transport section on page 162.

Although some hardy souls in the Long Distance Walkers Association are planning to walk the whole Capital Ring in one go, most people will take it in easy stages, so that the route will become a series of linear walks. For most Londoners, this will involve travelling out and back from home each time. Visitors are also likely to find it more practical to base themselves in reasonably central accommodation, travelling as above, rather than moving to new lodgings each night, though this could be arranged.

# SAFETY FIRST

The route has been designed to minimise road walking, but inevitably much of it follows or crosses some busy roads — in this book they can be identified by an 'A' or 'B' followed by a number. When crossing any road, common sense should of course prevail: you should only cross when it is safe to do so. Where possible, the route uses controlled or protected crossings, but there are a few places where a short diversion to a controlled crossing is advisable — attention is drawn to these in the route description. There are just a couple of spots where no crossing is available and extra care is therefore needed. The London Walking Forum is lobbying for more protected crossings along the route where necessary.

The description suggests which side of the road to follow where this helps you to cross an approaching major road at a protected point, or reduces the number of road crossings. The route goes through a few golf courses, where you should watch out for stray flying golf balls, especially when crossing a fairway. Always allow golfers to finish their stroke if your passing might disturb their concentration.

*The 14th-century tower of All Saints is all that remains of Isleworth's old parish church, following an act of wartime vandalism (Walk 7).*

# ACCESSIBILITY

Much of the route should be accessible to people using wheelchairs or buggies, but what may or may not be accessible will depend on individual circumstances. As a guide, Walks 4, 5, 7, 11, 13, 14 and 15 are mostly on a firm, level surface, though there are some exceptions. The other walks include some stretches that may be accessible. Elsewhere, steps, steep gradients, grass or uneven surfaces may make progress difficult or impossible. Where a practical alternative has been identified, this is also described. For each walk there is a general description under the heading 'Surface and terrain', which, together with the route description, should enable readers to judge its suitability.

# POINTS OF INTEREST

The author has tried to identify as many points of interest along the route as possible, but due to limitations of space it has not been practical to delve too deeply. Much of the history is common to the whole area. Prior to the Roman period, it was populated by mainly nomadic Celtic tribes, most of whom knuckled under and became Romanised, building villas and settlements close to roads out of London. If it had been invented before the formation of the County of London in 1888 and that of Greater London in 1965, the Capital Ring would have passed through the counties of Kent, Surrey, Middlesex and Essex, dating from Saxon times. Most of the towns and villages have names that are modified versions of the original Saxon settlements, established between the eighth century AD and the Norman Conquest in 1066.

The coming of the railways during the 19th century greatly affected the whole area, leading to a massive migration to more comfortable dwellings in what would henceforth be known as 'the suburbs' or 'the commuter belt'. It is to the everlasting credit of more enlightened citizens at that time that so much open space was saved from housing development for the walkers of today. Most of the parks and open spaces you pass through are owned by the appropriate London borough, though there are some exceptions, to which attention is drawn in the text.

# 1 WOOLWICH TO FALCONWOOD

**Distance**: 6.2 miles (10 km). Excludes Capital Ring links at each end: Woolwich Arsenal 0.6 miles (0.9 km); Falconwood 0.3 miles (0.5 km).

**Public transport.** The start of Walk 1 is 200 yards from bus stops in Hare Street. It is around half a mile from Woolwich Arsenal Station and more buses in General Gordon Place, and half a mile from North Woolwich Station and bus stops via the Woolwich Foot Tunnel or Woolwich Free Ferry. There are links en route with Woolwich Dockyard Station and Thames Barrier Pier. The finish is about 500 yards from Falconwood Station and bus stops. All places on this walk are in Travelcard and Bus Zone 4, except Woolwich Dockyard, Woolwich Road and Charlton, which are in Zone 3.

**Surface and terrain.** Woolwich to Woolwich Road: level paving or tarmac with some short, gentle slopes and two flights of steps (alternative ramp nearby). Woolwich Road to Charlton Park Road: some steep ascents and descents, mostly on paving or tarmac but with one short earth path; includes one very long upward flight of steps, which can be avoided along a signed diversion. Charlton Park Road to Shooters Hill: mostly level paving or tarmac but some avoidable grass and earth paths with gentle descents across Woolwich Common. Shooters Hill to Falconwood: mostly uneven paths and tracks, which may be muddy in places, with some long and fairly steep ascents and one long downward flight of steps (with signed avoiding diversion).

**Refreshments.** Woolwich, Woolwich Road, Old Charlton, Shooters Hill, Oxleas Meadows and Falconwood.

**Toilets.** Woolwich, Maryon Park, Charlton Park and Oxleas Meadows.

*Capital Ring link from Woolwich Arsenal Station and bus stops (0.6 miles/ 0.9 km). From the station exit **A**, bear half-right past the taxi stand and cross New Road. Go ahead past bus stops along the right-hand side of the square (General Gordon Place). Turn right along Greens End, with the market place (Beresford Square) ahead. In 50 yards turn left along partly pedestrianised Powis Street **B**. In 300 yards bear right along Hare Street **C**, past bus stops. At the end cross Woolwich High Street **D** and go clockwise (to your left) around the Waterfront Leisure Centre, turning right into Glass Yard, then right at its end to the circular red-brick structure that forms the exit from the Woolwich Foot Tunnel **E**. Or for toilets you can go anticlockwise, turning left along Bell Water Gate, then left at its end to the foot tunnel.*

*If you prefer to travel to North Woolwich Station **F**, from the exit turn right for 100 yards and go through the Woolwich Foot Tunnel (see Walk 15), or you can use the Woolwich Free Ferry.*

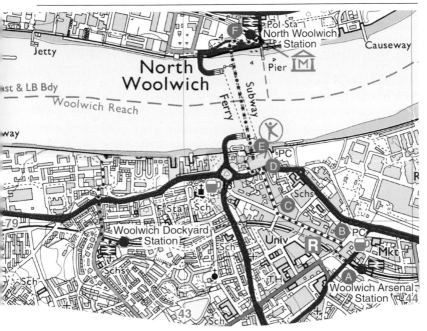

The history of Woolwich can be traced back to pre-Roman times, with evidence of an Iron Age (Celtic) settlement near the present ferry terminal. The Romans occupied a fortified encampment in the hills to the west, then the Saxons returned to the riverside to establish a fishing village, with the strange spelling Uuluuich (probably meaning 'wool harbour'); this was before the existence of the letter W. The Royal Naval Dockyard in 1512 was the first of several major institutions to be established here, the others being the Royal Arsenal (1545), the Royal Military Academy (1721) and the Woolwich Equitable Building Society ('The Woolwich', 1847). All have now closed down or moved away, though the building society still has several branches in the area. In 1886, some workers at the Royal Arsenal formed a football club known first as Dial Square, then Royal Arsenal, then Woolwich Arsenal, and finally plain Arsenal, but in 1913 it too moved away, to its current location in Highbury, North London.

Walk 1 of the Capital Ring starts beside the River Thames, at the south end of the Woolwich Foot Tunnel **E**, from which you should emerge triumphantly 75 miles (120 km) later on completing the route. The whole of Walk 1 keeps within the London Borough of Greenwich. By the tunnel exit, you will find the first of the Capital Ring's major signposts. It also carries the signs of two other routes with which the Ring shares its first mile. The sailing-barge logo denotes the south-east extension of the Thames Path. And you should watch out for cyclists, as this is also the Thames Cycle Route and National Cycle Route 1. In most places along this stretch, the Capital Ring logo has simply been added to the Thames Path signs. With your back to the tunnel exit and facing the river, go left along the brick roadway, bear left and then right, under a bridge, around the back of some buildings. At the top of a slope, bear left then immediately turn right across two sections of the approach road to the Woolwich Free Ferry. To your left, beyond the roundabout and Mitre pub, rises the tower of the 18th-century St Mary Magdalene Church. Turn right down the far side of the approach to the Woolwich Free Ferry **1**. It is likely that a ferry has existed here since the late 12th century. A toll was charged until 1889, then pressure from the people of Woolwich resulted in this being dropped, and the service has since been free, financed by various incarnations of the governing authority for London.

At the red ferry control cabin **G**, turn left beside a car park. Eventually, it is hoped that the route will go beside the river all the way to the Thames Barrier. For the moment, riverside access is unavailable at two points, and you must make two 'inland' diversions. The first starts beyond the car park, following a temporary tarmac path through land that was due to be redeveloped at the time of writing. For the next half-mile, the route passes through land that for four centuries was the Royal Naval Dockyard **2**, established in 1512 when the Great Harry was built here — King Henry VIII's flagship and the biggest warship of its time. The dockyard expanded and many other famous ships were launched here, including HMS *Beagle*, which from 1831 took five years to circumnavigate the globe with Charles Darwin on board as naturalist. Naval shipbuilding gradually moved to other locations, finally ceasing altogether in 1869, but the dockyard continued to be used for storage and administration until 1926, when it was sold to the Royal Arsenal Co-operative Society for warehousing. The land remained classified as secret, and depiction of the layout on maps was prohibited until fairly recently.

Continue along the riverside, here known as Resolution Walk. You now have a splendid vista ahead, encompassing in one line the Thames Barrier, the Millennium Dome, Canary Wharf and of course the Thames itself, while opposite is the extensive Tate & Lyle sugar refinery in Silvertown. You pass three small docks, formerly slipways and dry docks of the Royal Naval Dockyard, also known as graving or draw docks, built in the mid-19th century. Two of them are now stocked with fish for angling. A little further on, two unemployed

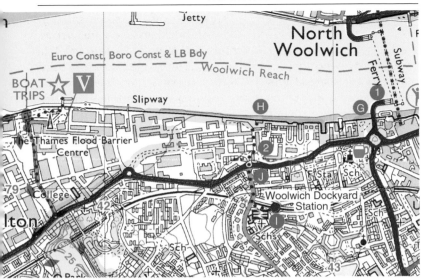

cannon pointing harmlessly across the river are remnants of the Gun Drill Battery **H** of the same era, used for training. To the left rises the Clockhouse of 1784, once the house and office of the Dockyard Admiral-Superintendent, now a community centre.

*Capital Ring link from Woolwich Dockyard Station (0.3 miles / 0.5 km).*
*From the main exit **I**, turn right along Belson Road, then right again down*
*Frances Street. Cross Woolwich Church Street **J** at the traffic lights then keep*
*ahead through the gateway into Leda Street. Turn left along Defiance Walk, past*
*the Clockhouse, and at the end climb the steps or ramp over the river wall to the*
*Gun Drill Battery **H** beside the River Thames. You join the Capital Ring by turning*
*left along the riverside.*

Closing in on the Thames Barrier, you pass a modern residential development known as Henry's Wharf, occupying the site of the Royal Naval Dockyard's Steam Factory, developed during the 1830s—1840s to build and maintain steam engines. Over to the left is its most visible remnant, a brick chimney almost 200 feet (60 metres) high. You come to a wall, part of the flood defences, which cannot be breached, so you must either climb over the steep steps — 18 up, 12 down — or use a ramp to the left. The steps form a graceful, white cantilevered structure, known as the Linkbridge, constructed in 2000 for Sustrans, the charity responsible for developing the National Cycle Network. The bridge doubles as a viewing platform, from which you have a fine view of the Thames Barrier.

*The view from Resolution Walk in Woolwich encapsulates modern London in a line: the*

*hames Barrier, the Millennium Dome and Canary Wharf.*

Any river in flood can pose huge problems for those who live and work nearby, but with the Thames the dangers are magnified out of all proportion by the huge amount of extra tidal water that surges upriver at certain times. This fact was driven home in 1953, when a particularly disastrous flood drowned over 300 people and caused immense damage. The eventual result was the construction of the Thames Flood Barrier **3**, popularly known as the Thames Barrier, completed in 1984. In times of flood danger, the gates are swung by electro-hydraulic power into an upright position between the piers; full closure of the barrier can be achieved in around 45 minutes.

Some 400 yards further on, the riverside walk comes to a temporary end **K**. Ahead now lies the site of the great Siemens factory, where submarine cables were made until 1968. Access through this area awaits redevelopment, so meanwhile you must leave the river, following signposts marked 'Thames Path Interim Route' through the Henry's Wharf area. Turn left and right behind a red-brick apartment block, then turn left and left again, so that you are now doubling back in an easterly direction along Harlinger Street. In 100 yards turn right along Ruston Road **L**, with the tall chimney ahead.

At the T-junction turn right, still in Ruston Road, past some commercial units, then bear left to the traffic roundabout **M**. Cross Warspite Road towards a café-bar and continue beside the dual carriageway A206 Woolwich Road. As you pass a set of pedestrian lights, opposite is St Catherine Laboure Catholic Church, while to your right is the green, copper-turreted Charlton Centre of Greenwich Community College, formerly Maryon Park School, built in 1896. Keep on to the next set of pedestrian lights, just before a tall, solid Environment Agency signboard **N** for the Thames Barrier.

*Capital Ring link with Thames Barrier and pier (0.4 miles / 0.7 km). There is an optional diversion here to see at close quarters the Thames Barrier, where there are a café and toilets in the Visitor Centre. To reach it, turn right immediately before the Environment Agency board, following Green Chain Walk signs through a narrow park. If you decide to travel to the Capital Ring by boat via Thames Barrier Pier **O** (limited services at present), you just follow the Green Chain Walk signs to Woolwich Road and cross over to Maryon Park.*

Cross at the lights by the Environment Agency board **N** and go ahead through the gate into Maryon Park **4**. The Capital Ring now parts company with the Thames Path and heads south and southwest with the Green Chain Walk (GCW) for the next 16 miles (26 km) to Crystal Palace Park. This wedge-shaped network, extending over 40 miles (64 km) through south-east London, links many

woods, commons and other open spaces. It is planned that many signs on this part of the Capital Ring will show the logos of both routes; however, initially you may find only GCW signs and marker posts in place (bearing the distinctive linked G-C logo).

Maryon Park and Maryon Wilson Park, which follows, take their name from the Maryon Wilson family, who lived at Charlton House. Both parks were part of Hanging Wood, which included a number of sandpits, the source of sand used as floor covering in the days before carpets became widely available. In one of the pits, some 500 yards to the right of the Capital Ring, is Charlton Athletic Football Club's ground, The Valley. The mostly landscaped Maryon Park was formed from another of the pits, donated by the Maryon Wilsons to London County Council in 1891. If you have seen Michelangelo Antonioni's 1966 movie *Blow-Up*, you may recognise this as the main location.

Ignoring the GCW alternative route to the right, turn left up the slope, then right at the top. Go past the playground and cross the railway line. At a path junction **P** the Capital Ring bears right to keep the tennis courts to your left. A very long flight of steps lies ahead. They can be avoided by following the signed GCW diversion to the

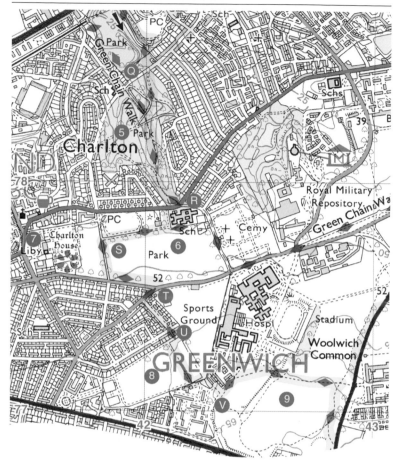

left here. In 200 yards take your time as you climb the 115 steps up to your right. *There are toilets 100 yards to the left from the foot of the steps.* At the top, go through a gate then bear right on a gravel path to Thorntree Road **Q**, and cross into Maryon Wilson Park **5**.

You descend quite steeply on tarmac paths, with two shallow steps, to pass between the pens of a children's zoo. Turn left and climb steadily up a pretty combe beside a winding little stream to emerge at Charlton Park Road **R**, opposite Charlton Park Special School. Turn right and cross the road at the pedestrian refuge, then in a few yards turn left into Charlton Park itself **6**. Walk along the drive, past a small car park and a barrier. Turn right along a tarmac path lined with lime trees, with Charlton House **7** ahead. Charlton

House is acknowledged as one of the best examples of a Jacobean building in London. It was completed in 1612 for Sir Adam Newton, tutor to Prince Henry, son of King James I. What are now known as Charlton Park, Maryon Park, Maryon Wilson Park and Hornfair Park were all part of the Charlton House estate. The house is now used as a community centre and library. The area between the house and its gates used to be the village green, where the Charlton Horn Fair took place from its origin in the 16th century until 1829, when the Maryon Wilsons enclosed the green. The fair continued on a nearby field, but was banned in 1872 following increasingly drunken and libidinous behaviour. It was revived in 1973, on the original site by the house, and now takes place on the last Sunday in June.

At the T-junction **S**, the Capital Ring turns left. *You may wish to visit Charlton House and take advantage of facilities in Old Charlton village: turn right towards a pavilion (toilets), then turn left before the gate.* With Charlton House to your right, note the ha-ha or sunken wall, intended to separate the house from the park without spoiling the view. Just before the road, turn left through a gap in the fence onto grass inside and parallel to the park fence – you can avoid the grass by walking along the pavement outside the park. In just over 200 yards leave the park through a small gate, which may be hidden in trees, on to Charlton Park Lane.

Turn right and shortly cross the road before a mini-roundabout **T** at the junction with Canberra Road. Turn right then immediately left along Inigo Jones Road, whose name marks a connection at Charlton House with the celebrated 17th-century architect. This leads ahead across Prince Henry Road **U** and along an alleyway into the rather bland Hornfair Park **8**. Originally known as Charlton Playing Fields, it was renamed in 1948 to commemorate the Horn Fair described above. Turn right then left along a gravel path, heading for a long, red-brick building. At the end, turn left along a narrow, loose-gravel path. Bear right through a gate and along a grassy path on to Baker Road **V**. Turn left and in 75 yards, just before the Queen Elizabeth Hospital in Stadium Road, go over a zebra crossing. Jink right between bollards then left along an earth path, diagonal to the road. This leads to a tarmac path, which you follow across Woolwich Common **9**.

During the 18th and 19th centuries, Woolwich Common was sometimes a scene of mass military activity. Before engaging in an overseas campaign, the British army would assemble and camp here before going to Woolwich Arsenal to collect their weaponry and embark on ships moored in the Thames. Behind the trees to your left is the site of Woolwich Stadium, from 1920 to 1973 the scene of many military sporting engagements. Crossing the open common, peeping above the foliage ahead are the parapets of the former Royal Military Academy **10**, with Shooters Hill rising behind it. Known to its graduates as 'The Shop', the academy was the precursor to the current one at Sandhurst, and replaced a much smaller one in the Royal Arsenal.

In the middle of the common, you cross a gravel track. At a path junction **W** just before the narrow strip of woodland, turn right along a dirt path. Walk beside the trees for 200 yards, then fork left onto Academy Road. A prominent red-brick tower away to your right, formerly a water tower, is now the centrepiece of a residential development. Turn right beside the road to the traffic lights at Shooters Hill **X**. Cross left at the lights over Academy Road, then right over Shooters Hill towards the police station. Stretching down the hill is the grey-brick former Royal Herbert Hospital, which served the military from 1865 to 1978; it is now converted into private apartments. Shooters Hill occupies part of the Roman Watling Street from Dover to London. The summit, at 432 feet (130 metres), is one of the highest points in Greater London.

*You could imagine yourself transported to the Alps as you approach the 'mountain hut' at the top of Oxleas Meadows.*

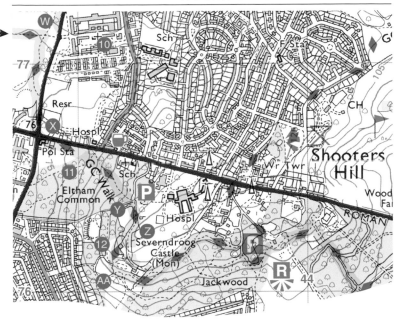

Turn left by the 'new' red-brick police station of 1915 and keep on past the original yellow-brick one of 1852. At the start of Eltham Common **11**, bear slightly right across grass, heading for a grassy inlet in the trees about 30 yards in from the road. Eltham Common is part of Shooters Hill Woods, a continuous belt of ancient woodland, together with Castlewood, Jackwood and Oxleas Wood, all traversed by the Capital Ring. They were acquired by the London County Council during the 1920s and 1930s, and have been designated a site of special scientific interest by the Nature Conservancy Council because of the many rare species of flora and fauna found there.

Continue in the same direction into Castle Wood, climbing quite steeply on a rough path. At the top, by a car park **Y**, turn right along an access road, where you pass an information board with an unusual relief map of the area. At a fork **Z**, keep ahead to the intriguingly named Severndroog Castle **12**, the highest point not only of Walk 1 but of the whole Capital Ring at altitude 404 feet (121 metres). The castle's strange name is taken from a fortress in India that was captured by Commodore Sir William James, who during the 18th century owned this land, then called Park Farm, later to become Eltham Park. After the commodore's death in 1784, his widow had the tower built as a memorial.

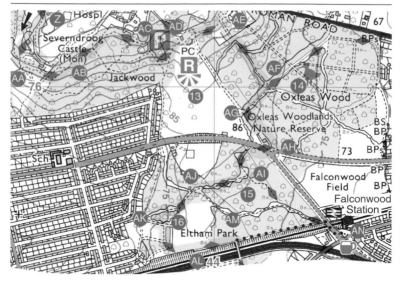

The rest of Walk 1 follows a rather complicated route, mostly in woodland, but well marked by GCW wooden posts. Beyond Severndroog, a path leads down to a flight of steps in several sections, with a total of about 70 steps. *These can be avoided on a GCW-signed alternative route, for which you should return to the fork **Z** just before Severndroog Castle, then turn sharp right down a tarmac track. If you follow this alternative, skip the next paragraph to rejoin the main route by keeping ahead at the path junction **AB**.*

Continuing down the steps on the main route, you reach a fork, where you can go either left or right. Go down more steps and keep ahead across a terrace, formerly the rose garden of Castlewood House, which stood here from the 1870s to the 1920s. On the far side go down yet more steps, then turn left at the foot along a level path on top of a disused reservoir **AA**. Pass through a gap in a wall into Jackwood. You cross Stone Alley, an ancient track linking Shooters Hill with Eltham, then bear half-left up a slope, and turn left at the top. At the next junction **AB**, turn right.

Go downhill to cross a small stream or ditch, then up again to join a tarmac path. At a fork, bear right along the lower of two paths through a grassed area, with a wall up to your left. This is the former ornamental garden of Jackwood House, which from the 1860s to the 1920s sat on what are now flowerbeds to your left. Bear left at the end of the gardens, then turn right at the next junction **AC** to descend through more woodland and emerge into Oxleas Meadows **13**. Bear left up to a pavilion **AD**, which sits atop the hill like an alpine mountain hut. It contains toilets and a café, from which you can admire the extensive view across south-east London to the North Downs.

Keep ahead past the pavilion and again at the tarmac path junction. Where the tarmac ends, keep ahead on the main rising track into Oxleas Wood **14**. Passing a massive tree with four great trunks **AE**, fork right downhill. In 25 yards, fork right again, deeper into the woods, ignoring side turnings, to reach a GCW signpost **AF** at a junction. Turn right along a broad, often muddy track, and in 150 yards, with the grass of Oxleas Meadows to your right, turn left **AG**. In 100 yards fork left to reach Welling Way. Turn right to cross ahead at the lights over Rochester Way **AH**.

Go ahead on a narrow earth path into the trees of Eltham Park North **15**, here known as Shepherdleas Wood. In a few yards, turn right, parallel with the road, for 75 yards, then turn left, and in another 75 yards turn left again to a GCW junction signpost **AI**, which may be hidden in the foliage on the left. Turn right here, then at a major crossing track **AJ** keep ahead on a path that bends left, with an open space to your left. Descend among trees to a junction, where you turn left into an open space. On reaching a tarmac path **AK**, turn left along it then shortly turn right beside the railings of Long Pond **16**, once a boating lake, now a quiet retreat for waterbirds, with good views towards the City of London and Crystal Palace.

At the end of the pond, bear left, still on a tarmac path, to follow a high fence. The roar of traffic has been increasing steadily, and its source lies to your right in the shape of the A2 Rochester Way Relief Road, occasionally augmented by trains on the Dartford Loop line, out of sight in a cutting below. When the tarmac finishes, jink right past a wooden railing **AL**, then left along a wide, rolled-earth track in woodland, still beside the fence. In 200 yards you reach the wide, concrete Green Link Bridge **AM**, where Walk 1 of the Capital Ring ends. *To continue on Walk 2, turn right across the bridge into Eltham Park South.*

**Capital Ring link to Falconwood Station and bus stops** *(0.3 mile / 0.5 km).*
*Do not cross the bridge but continue ahead beside the railway for 400 yards to Rochester Way. Turn right across the railway and cross at the lights to Falconwood Station **AN** and bus stops.*

# 2 FALCONWOOD TO GROVE PARK

**Distance**: 3.4 miles (5.4 km). Excludes Capital Ring links at each end: 0.3 miles (0.5 km) from Falconwood and 0.4 miles (0.7 km) to Grove Park.

**Public transport.** The start of Walk 2 is 500 yards from Falconwood Station and bus stops. There is a link en route with Mottingham Station. The finish is 200 yards from bus stops and just under half a mile from Grove Park Station. All places on this walk are in Travelcard and Bus Zone 4.

**Surface and terrain.** From Falconwood Station to the start on the Green Link Bridge is mostly on a level, rolled-earth path. Green Link Bridge to Eltham: mostly level paving or tarmac, with a short stretch on an earth path. Eltham to Middle Park: mostly gentle descent on a dirt track. Middle Park to Grove Park: mostly level paving or tarmac, but with 700 yards on an earth path and a stepped footbridge over a railway line.

**Refreshments:** Falconwood, Eltham and Grove Park.

**Toilets.** Eltham Park South, Eltham and Grove Park.

*Capital Ring link from Falconwood Station and bus stops (0.3 mile / 0.5 km).*
*From Falconwood Station exit **A** turn right along Lingfield Crescent and cross Rochester Way at the refuge. Ignore Green Chain Walk (GCW) signs to the left. Turn right to cross the railway, then turn left at the GCW signs along a rolled-earth path beside the railway into woodland in Eltham Park North. In 450 yards you reach a wide concrete bridge. You join the Capital Ring by turning left here.*

Walk 2 starts at the Green Link Bridge **B** in the London Borough of Greenwich, and you are still sharing the route of the Green Chain Walk (GCW). The bridge leads over the railway line and A2 Rochester Way Relief Road into Eltham Park South **1**. This is an open and formal park, in complete contrast to the wooded and more natural Eltham Park North on Walk 1. Turn right at the GCW fingerpost, then immediately left to follow the tarmac path along the left-hand side of the park, with Eltham Warren Golf Course beyond the fence. *There are toilets in the red-brick building away to the right by some tennis courts.*

At the end of the park, cross then turn left along Glenesk Road **C**, near the site of the former mansion of Eltham Park. In 250 yards cross the busy A210 Bexley Road **D** at the refuge. Continue ahead along a concrete track called Butterfly Lane — take care, as it has no pavement and can be busy with vehicles at times, being the approach to stables and the Tudor Sports and Social Club. At the

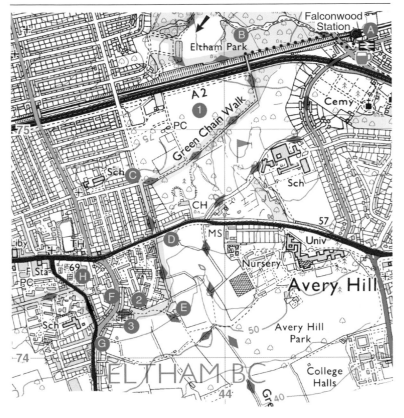

club gate **E**, bear right along an earth path to a triangular patch of grass with a GCW junction signpost. Bear right into Conduit Meadows and shortly you pass an odd little brick structure, which is Conduit Head **2**. Surprisingly unprotected, it is in fact a Grade II listed building, which once housed sluices to control the flow of water from springs nearby to Eltham Palace. Continue ahead between fences to Southend Crescent, with Holy Trinity Church **3** on your left. Consecrated in 1869, it contains the Gallipoli Chapel, a memorial to those who died in the World War I battle of that name. If you hear heavenly voices, it will probably be Eltham Choral Society, who perform regular concerts here.

Turn left along Southend Crescent **F**, then at the mini-roundabout **G** cross right then immediately left over Footscray Road. Turn right up the left-hand side of Footscray Road, passing St Thomas More Roman Catholic Comprehensive School. In 200 yards the Capital Ring goes left along North Park **H**. *For toilets go ahead to the garage* *and turn left along Messeter Place.* Along the left-hand side of North Place, in 500 yards you pass Passey Place **I**, the nearest point to the facilities of Eltham High Street. The town seems to breed great comics: it has a theatre named after Bob Hope, who was born here in 1903 but emigrated with his family to the United States at the age of four, and Frankie Howerd spent much of his childhood here.

At the end of North Park, cross Court Road **J** at the refuge to the left, then continue in the same direction along an earth pavement on the left-hand side of Tilt Yard Approach. At a grass area, where the original gatehouse to Eltham Palace was situated, cross over and turn left along Court Yard **K**, which used to be an outer courtyard of the palace. Just before the present palace gate **L**, on your right, is a mustard-and-black timber-framed building, dating from the early 16th century, which was the Lord Chancellor's Lodgings **4** — occasional residents included Cardinal Wolsey and Sir Thomas More. It has been converted into three houses: number 34 was the Parlour, 36 the Hall, and 38 the Great Chamber. Directly ahead now, across a moat, lies the Great Hall of Eltham Palace **5**, the principal country residence of the English monarchy for nearly 250 years, from the early 14th to the mid-16th centuries. It was surrounded by an extensive deer park and became a favourite resort for hunting. The Great Hall, with its impressive hammerbeam roof, was added during the 1470s, but Henry VIII lost interest in Eltham, instead favouring Greenwich and Hampton Court. During the Civil War, the palace and gardens were ransacked and ruined by Cromwell's troops. In the 1930s, the palace was acquired by the Courtauld family, of textiles fame. They built a flamboyant new mansion for their own use, restored part of the moat, and created beautiful gardens. They moved out during World War II, and the hall was used as a military college until 1992. English Heritage have since restored the whole complex as a tourist attraction and function venue.

From the gate of Eltham Palace, turn right down King John's Walk, a road with no pavement, so take care, especially at the bends. Near the foot of the hill, at a GCW signpost beside a footpath junction **M**, turn left, still on the tarmac road with no pavement. There are good views from here across South London and towards the City of London. Where the tarmac ends, by stables, keep ahead past a barrier on a rough, gently rising track between fields — still King John's Walk. Look back now for a grand view of Canary Wharf behind the yellow masts of the Millennium Dome. At the brow, in Middle Park now, you reach another GCW junction signpost. Continue down to and cross Middle Park Avenue to reach a grassed area **N**.

***Capital Ring link with Mottingham Station*** *(0.5 mile / 0.8 km). Turn left along Middle Park Avenue all the way to Court Road* **O**, *where you turn right to Mottingham Station* **P**. *If starting here, from the station's main exit go up the approach road, then at the main road turn left over the railway. In 70 yards turn left again along Middle Park Avenue* **O**. *Ignore GCW signs in this area. In 800 yards, halfway along a grass area (Joan Crescent)* **N**, *turn left along a concrete-lined path to join the Capital Ring.*

Keep ahead along a concrete-lined path. This leads to a footbridge over a railway line, with 35 steps up and down. Cross with great care the A20 Sidcup Road **Q**, which has no controlled crossing, but there is a central reservation. Continue ahead along a tarmac path between houses and a horse-riding field, crossing the boundary for a brief first visit to the London Borough of Bromley. In 200 yards you reach a GCW junction signpost on Mottingham Lane **R**. Cross over then turn right along the far side for 450 yards. On your right is Mottingham Farm **6**, which around the turn of the 20th century was the home of Farmer Brown, a local character who adopted the typical farmer's

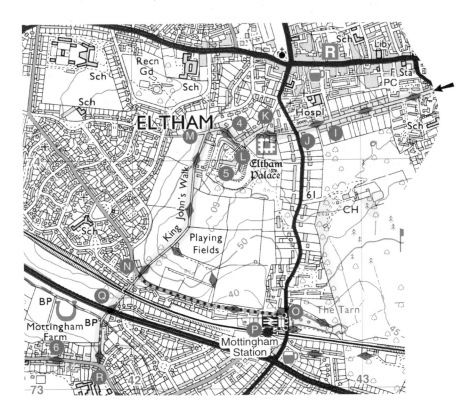

*The moat at Eltham Palace, dating from the 14th century, was restored by the Courtauld family in the 1930s.*

garb of smock and tall hat, and set a fine example by living to 102 on a diet of whisky, ale, steak and cigars. Further on, past Eltham College Junior School and just before a right-hand bend, the route goes left along a footpath **S**, but walk on for 30 yards to see Fairmount **7**, a large house on the right. Now a residential home for the elderly, it was formerly the home of supreme cricketer W.G. Grace, as indicated on the blue plaque.

The narrow earth footpath runs straight at first, between paddocks on your right and, on your left, the playing fields of Eltham College, whose flag-topped tower **8** rises beyond. Former pupils of the college include Eric Liddell, the athlete of *Chariots of Fire* fame, and Mervyn Peake, author of the *Gormenghast* trilogy. This path can get very muddy after heavy rain, and is calf-deep in fallen leaves in late autumn and winter. It turns right then left between more paddocks and playing fields, the latter belonging to the City of London Sports & Social Club. You come to a railing, where the path bears left **T**. In a concrete channel below is the infant Quaggy River **9**, a tributary of the Ravensbourne. At a sports pavilion, bear right along its access road, which crosses into the London Borough of Lewisham, to a GCW junction signpost on Marvels Lane **U**, the end of Walk 2. *To continue on to Walk 3, turn right along Marvels Lane.*

**Capital Ring link to Grove Park Station** *(0.4 mile / 0.7 km). Carefully cross Marvels Lane and keep ahead along a footpath beside the Quaggy River. At Chinbrook Road go over the zebra crossing **V** then turn right uphill. At the top turn left to Grove Park Station **W**, with bus stops nearby.*

# 3 GROVE PARK TO CRYSTAL PALACE

**Distance**: 8.2 miles (13.2 km). Excludes Capital Ring link of 0.4 miles (0.7 km) from Grove Park Station to the start.

**Public transport**. The start of Walk 3 is in Marvels Lane, just under half a mile from Grove Park Station and bus station. Buses serve Chinbrook Road, 200 yards from the start. The route passes New Beckenham and Penge East Stations, and there are links with Ravensbourne and Penge West Stations. The walk finishes at Crystal Palace Station, close to bus stops. All places on this walk are in Travelcard and Bus Zone 4.

**Surface and terrain**. Grove Park to Downham: mostly level paving or tarmac, with one stepped footbridge. Downham to New Beckenham: mostly on tarmac or rolled-earth paths or tracks through Beckenham Place Park with short ascents and descents, sometimes steep. New Beckenham to Penge: level tarmac or paving with one stepped footbridge. Penge to Crystal Palace Park: tarmac or paving with some short steep ascents and descents. The route climbs steadily inside Crystal Palace Park.

**Refreshments**. Grove Park, Downham, Beckenham Place Park, Penge, Crystal Palace Park, Anerley Hill.

**Toilets**. Grove Park, Downham, Beckenham Place Park, Crystal Palace Park.

*Capital Ring link from Grove Park Station (0.4 miles / 0.7 km). From the station exit **A** turn right along Baring Road. At the traffic lights turn right down Chinbrook Road. At the foot of the hill, go left over the zebra crossing and keep ahead along a footpath beside the Quaggy River. In 200 yards at Marvels Lane **B**, turn left along the left-hand pavement, with Walk 2 of the Capital Ring coming in along the drive opposite. Cross over at the refuge, then continue in the same direction on the far side. You join the Capital Ring here.*

Walk 3 of the Capital Ring starts in Marvels Lane **B** in the London Borough of Lewisham, still keeping company with the Green Chain Walk (GCW). Pass the former Grove Park Hospital, now being re-developed as a residential area. After a group of trees marking one end of Sydenham Cottages Nature Reserve, turn right past Grove Park Library. Cross Somertrees Avenue **C** at the refuge, turn right then immediately left along the left-hand side of Coopers Lane. In 250 yards you reach the A2212 Baring Road **D**. Turn right and cross at the second refuge. Turn right then immediately left along a tarmac footpath called Railway Children Walk **1** after the famous book by E. Nesbitt (Mrs Edith Bland), who lived nearby. Shortly, you pass Hither Green Nature Reserve **2**. Among the unusual species that

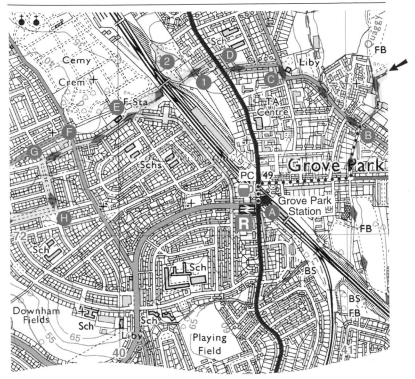

can be spotted here are green ring-necked parakeets, though these are becoming a fairly common sight in London's open spaces.

Cross the footbridge (24 steps) over the main railway line from London to the Kent coast. *To avoid the bridge, from Grove Park Station go ahead along Downham Way, then take the first right, Reigate Road, for 700 yards to meet the footpath off the bridge at the third left-hand bend E.* A major rail disaster occurred to the right of the bridge in 1967, when a derailment resulted in 49 fatalities. Continue along the footpath through a landscaped area, with Hither Green Cemetery to your right. At Reigate Road **E** keep ahead along the right-hand pavement, passing a children's playground and Downham Fire Station with its training tower. At the main road, Verdant Lane **F**, cross via the central reservation. Keep ahead along Whitefoot Terrace, then in 150 yards turn left up Woodbank Road **G**. This has two roadways on either side of a grassy, wooded central strip, and you can walk either on the grass or along the right-hand pavement. Pass Bideford and Ilfracombe Roads, then turn right along Undershaw Road **H**, with a similar strip separating it from Shaw Road. At the end, cross

Moorside Road **I** and go ahead along a tarmac footpath which is the Downham Woodland Walk **3**, where dogs should be kept on a lead. The Downham Woodland Walk runs for over a mile along a narrow strip of woodland, a remnant of the Great North Wood. Until London began to expand, this vast forest stretched some 7 miles along the hills between what are now Croydon and Deptford, and you will encounter other remnants further along the Capital Ring.

The Woodland Walk crosses several roads. At the first, Downderry Road **J**, continue to the left of a postbox and railings beside some cottages to re-enter the wood. At this point, you cross the Greenwich Meridian Line and then closely follow it for 400 yards — it will be encountered again on Walk 14. The path now winds between houses and crosses Oakshade Road **K** and Haddington Road **L**. At the end of the path, cross Oakridge Road to the A21 Bromley Road **M** at Downham.

Go over the zebra crossing, then turn half-left along Old Bromley Road, crossing to the right-hand pavement. *At Downham Way **N**, there is an automatic toilet at the main road to your left.* Cross Brangbourne Road, then after 50 yards turn right through the entrance **O** into Beckenham Place Park **4**, once the private estate of Beckenham Place (see below). This very large park has open grassland in this corner, but becomes well wooded later. Follow the tarmac footpath along the right-hand edge, shortly crossing a humped footbridge. Below it is the River Ravensbourne **5**, flowing from Keston Ponds, near Bromley, through Catford and Lewisham to the Thames at Deptford Creek. Its name is supposed to derive from Roman times, when Caesar's army camped near Keston: soldiers searching for water saw ravens frequenting a certain spot and discovered a spring there.

In 250 yards the Capital Ring turns sharp left at a path junction **P** in a copse. *At this point, you can continue ahead for 300 yards to Beckenham Hill Station **Q**, though this is not a formal Capital Ring link.* The path bends right up a ramp to cross a railway line. The tarmac peters out as you bear left beside Beckenham Place Park Golf Course to continue on a gravel path. In 200 yards fork right, ignoring turnings into the golf course. In another 200 yards at a T-junction **R**, turn right and climb steadily up a track, which may be muddy, for 150 yards to a path intersection **S**. A GCW alternative route avoiding imminent steps continues ahead, but the Capital Ring follows its main route to the right, leading in 125 fairly steep yards with some widely spaced steps to a GCW junction signpost **T** and information board at the centre of Beckenham Place Park, where you bear right.

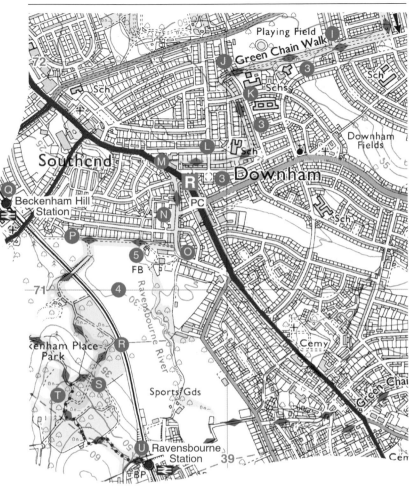

***Capital Ring link with Ravensbourne Station*** *(0.5 miles / 0.8 km). This follows a branch of the GCW, with its wooden marker posts. Turn left at the GCW signpost **T**, and shortly keep ahead past another one. In 80 yards fork left, then in 70 yards turn right. At an open space turn left along a tarmac path, and back in the trees turn right down a dirt track. At the road turn left to Ravensbourne Station **U**. If starting here, from the station exit turn left along an unmade road, then in 60 yards turn right into Beckenham Place Park. Follow the GCW marker posts ahead up an earth track. At a T-junction turn left on a tarmac path into an open space. Just before a brick building, turn right into the wood, then turn left at the path junction. In 30 yards turn right and keep ahead past a GCW signpost. In 70 yards the track bears left to another GCW signpost **T** at the centre of the park, where you join the Capital Ring by keeping ahead beyond the sign.*

*John Cator's 18th-century mansion in Beckenham Place Park.*

Pass a golf green then keep ahead past a tee, swinging left on loose gravel. You descend to cross a little stream and join a tarmac path, which rises towards the mansion. On your right are a white-painted giant squirrel sculpture and the clocktower of the former stable block — the flower beds here are worth a very short diversion. You come to a path junction **V**, immediately before the mansion, which is Beckenham Place **6**. *There are public toilets just before it.* The park and an earlier mansion were acquired in 1773 by John Cator, a wealthy timber merchant. He rebuilt the mansion, incorporating bits of his previous home, Wricklemarsh Park, near Blackheath, including the splendid portico. The mansion and park were acquired for public use in 1927 by London County Council. They developed the public golf course, with its clubhouse and cafeteria in the mansion, now a Grade II listed building.

Turn right through a gap in the bushes to a driveway, then turn left beside a car park. With the grand portico of the mansion on your left, turn right along a tarmac path. This swings right then left to lead out of the park on to a road **W** — Beckenham Hill to your right, Southend Road to your left. Now back in the London Borough of Bromley, turn left along A2105 Southend Road for 200 yards. Cross over at the

refuge just before Calverley Close and continue along the far pavement to the junction with Stumps Hill Lane **X**, where you turn right.

Where Stumps Hill Lane becomes unmade, keep ahead down a
stretch with no pavement. The Capital Ring now threads a route
between the fringes of Beckenham to your left and Sydenham to
your right. Ahead is the handsome pavilion of Lloyds Bank Sports
Club, and you have a fine view beyond it towards Crystal Palace,
where this walk ends. At the foot, cross Worsley Bridge Road **Y** to the
GCW fingerpost and turn left. Away to the right, the roof of another
imposing pavilion proudly proclaims 'Crystal Palace FC', for this is the
training ground of that historic football club. At the T-junction **Z** cross
Brackley Road and turn right.

***Capital Ring link with Beckenham Junction Station and Croydon Tramlink***
*(0.6 miles / 0.9 km). Turn left up Brackley Road, then turn right at the top along
Southend Road. In 600 yards, at traffic lights, turn right along Rectory Road then
immediately right again along the approach to Beckenham Junction Station **AA**
and tram stop. If starting here, from the main station exit go ahead to Rectory
Road, turn left to the traffic lights and left again over the railway line. Continue
ahead along Southend Road, then in 600 yards turn left down Brackley Road. You
join the Capital Ring by keeping ahead at the junction with Worsley Bridge Road **Z**.*

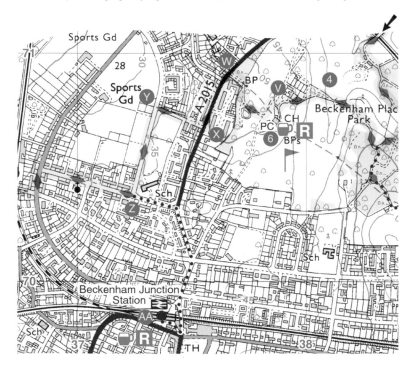

You are now heading for the stately spire of St Paul's Church **7**, New Beckenham. At the end of Brackley Road, cross Copers Cope Road **AB**, named after a large farm that once occupied this area. Turn left, then shortly turn right along Park Road to pass through a ramped subway **AC** under New Beckenham Station. The original station lay to the left; it was replaced by the current one, to the right, in 1904.

You emerge from the subway for the first of three brief encounters with the long and straight Lennard Road. With the HSBC Sports & Social Club on your right, in 50 yards turn left into King's Hall Road **AD**, using the right-hand pavement. In 275 yards, opposite Bridge Road **AE**, turn right between house numbers 173 and 175 along a tarmac path into Cator Park **8**, formerly the private Kent House Pleasure Gardens. You cross two streams — The Beck, then Chaffinch Brook — which merge a little way to your right, inside the park, to form the Pool River, a tributary of the Ravensbourne. At the GCW signpost **AF** at the centre of the park, you come to a shared-use track for cyclists and pedestrians, where you turn right. This is part of the Waterlink Way, developed by Sustrans, from the Thames at Deptford Creek through South London into Surrey.

*Capital Ring link with Kent House Station (0.2 miles/ 0.4 km). At the signpost, bear half-left out of Cator Park. Cross and turn left along Aldersmead Road, then cross Kings Hall Road at the refuge. Turn left along the unmade Kent House Station Approach and go through the subway* **AG** *to the station platforms. If starting here, from the platforms follow signs to Kings Hall Road, where you turn right, then left along Aldersmead Road to enter Cator Park. At the central GCW signpost* **AF***, turn left past the wooden pavilion onto the Capital Ring.*

*In Cator Park the Capital Ring briefly joins the Waterlink Way cycle path.*

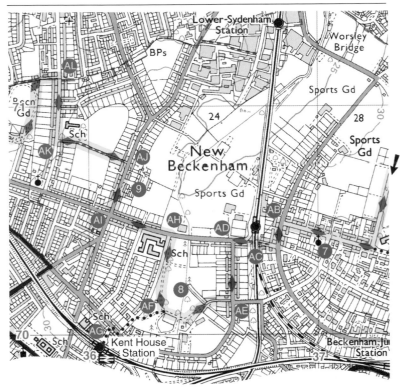

Continue along the shared-use track to the point where it turns right, then keep ahead to the corner of the park and back onto Lennard Road **AH**, dominated here by Cator Park Girls School. A route diversion is planned here that will lead through an open space ahead, but in the meantime you turn left and go over the zebra crossing, then keep ahead to the traffic lights **AI**. Cross over then turn right along Kent House Road. About 100 yards along on your right, Beckett Walk covers the site of Kent House **9**, which gave its name to the area and the station. The name resulted from it being at one time the first building in Kent on the road out of London. It dated from the 13th century and through most of its existence was a farmhouse. In the early 20th century, it became a nursing home, which was demolished in 1957.

In a further 100 yards, between house numbers 148 and 150, turn left along a narrow, fenced footpath **AJ** leading between school playing fields to Cator Road **AK**. Cross over, then turn right for 275 yards, passing Woodbastwick Road. Just past number 57 (The Woodfields) **AL**, this becomes Trewsbury Road as it crosses into the

*A sphinx gazes over Crystal Palace Park beneath the towering television mast, on the site of the great building that burned down in 1936.*

London Borough of Lewisham; however, you just about stay in Bromley by turning left along an unmade driveway. At the end, turn left along a tarmac path along the left-hand side of Alexandra Recreation Ground **10**, opened to the public in 1891 and named after Queen Alexandra, wife of King Edward VII. At a dilapidated toilet block, turn right between a bowling green and a disused drinking fountain. Pass a house inside the park, then turn left into Maitland Road **AM**, keeping ahead along its left-hand side.

At the end, for the third time, is Lennard Road **AN**, now much busier as part of the A213. At present, there is no easy crossing point, so, with great care, cross over then turn right over Parish Lane, or turn right to cross Lennard Road halfway to the bend. At the next junction (Newlands Park), turn left to cross the footbridge (25 steps) at Penge East Station **AO**. *To avoid this bridge, from Maitland Road keep ahead along Parish Lane, then in 250 yards turn right along Penge Lane. Take the first right, Queen Adelaide Road, then right at St John's Road to Penge East Station **AO**. Continue ahead past the footbridge along Station Road.* Here you may see Eurostar trains travelling between Waterloo and the Channel Tunnel. Looking left as you cross the footbridge, the building that protrudes into the far platform used to be the cottage of the keeper of the level crossing which once linked the roads on either side. On the far side, take the right-hand steps down to the station forecourt. Turn right along Station Road, with the dainty little Church of the Good Shepherd and Our Lady **11** opposite, established at the turn of the 20th century as a mission house (with no incumbent of its own). In 200 yards turn left along Kingswood Road **AP**, following the right-hand pavement to A234 Penge High Street **AQ**, where you cross at the lights. The name Penge is unusual for this area, having a Celtic origin — Penceat or Pencoed, meaning wood end.

Turn right up Penge High Street to pass under two railway bridges **AR**. The first carries the main line from London Bridge to the Sussex coast. This section was one of the earliest railway lines in London, built in 1839 for the London and Croydon Railway. It was originally operated by atmospheric traction, by which trains were vacuum-drawn through a continuous pipe. The second bridge was built in 1854 for the branch to Crystal Palace.

*Capital Ring link with Penge West Station (0.1 miles / 0.1 km). Between the bridges **AR**, turn left along Anerley Road to find Penge West Station **AS** on your left. If starting here, from the station exit go ahead to the road then turn right along Anerley Road. At Penge High Street turn left under the second bridge **AR**.*

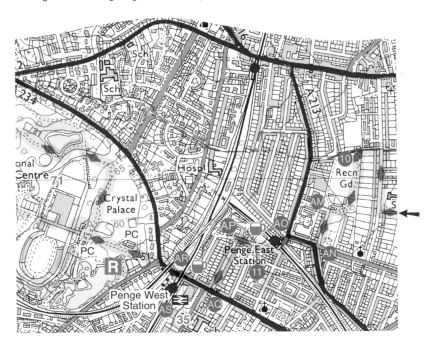

Cross Thicket Road and go through the Penge entrance **AT** into Crystal Palace Park **12**. Keep ahead past a car park to a park signpost **AU**, with an information centre and toilets to your right and a café to your left. The Green Chain Walk finishes here, and at last the Capital Ring strikes out on its own. Crystal Palace Park was created in 1854 to provide a new site for the great glass exhibition hall that had previously stood in Hyde Park for the Great Exhibition of 1851. The Crystal Palace became the focus of the world's first theme park, offering a fantastic array of displays, circuses, concerts and shows. But although it was one of the most popular tourist attractions of its day, it never recovered its costs. In 1911, the Crystal Palace Company was declared bankrupt, and two years later the palace became the property of the nation. Then, in 1936, the building was completely destroyed by a spectacular fire, and the site and terraces at the top of the park have since lain desolate. Crystal Palace Park is now managed by the London Borough of Bromley, who recently carried out a substantial regeneration scheme, improving the lakes, landscaping and famous collection of dinosaur sculptures. It is hoped that a smaller version of the Crystal Palace will eventually be constructed on the original site.

The Capital Ring originally went up to the left, past the lakes, through what is now a prehistoric display area **13**. Guided tours are available and well worth an hour's diversion — details can be obtained from the information centre. The present route follows a circuitous but interesting route around the east and north sides of the park. A diversion is some-times necessary during events and will be signed when in use. Continue ahead up the central avenue, where London plane trees replace Paxton's original conifers. At the next park signpost **AV**, the main route turns right.

*If the diversion mentioned above is in force, you must pass the sign-post then bear half-right to climb 22 steps, turn sharp left, then climb right up 22 more steps to continue in the same direction along the park's central axis, slicing through the National Sports Centre **14**. To your left is the athletics stadium, to your right the swimming pool, while underneath is an indoor sprint track. Keep ahead past a bust of Paxton to a crossing track **AY**, where you turn left to rejoin the main route. The steps can be avoided by keeping ahead into the National Sports Centre, turning left along the service road, under a bridge, and on to the exit **AZ**.*

The main route follows a path with open grass to your right and a rising bank to your left. You pass the ship's bell from the SS *Crystal Palace*, a World War II memorial in its own little pavilion, to fork left on another track as you approach the Sydenham Gate. Now in wood-land, you pass through a gate **AW** and turn right uphill, then very soon sharp left to pass a fishing lake on your right. Beyond that, a path

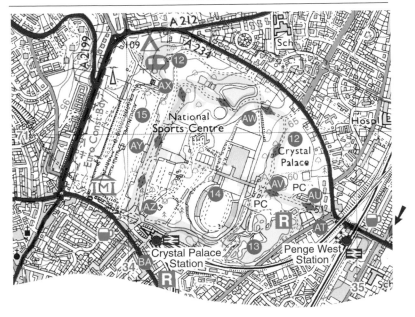

leads off to the left into The Maze. Opposite, another path leads into a rhododendron dell. Looming ahead now is the rusted iron, cantilevered hulk of the concert stage, with a moat to protect artistes from their adoring fans, for this is the scene in summer of regular open-air concerts of both classical and pop music. At the next path junction **AX**, turn left along the lower of two paths, with lampposts. Pass through a gate to cross the central avenue **AY** again.

Up to your right now are the terraces **15**, where the great palace itself once stood. Above the terraces soars the Crystal Palace transmitter, beaming most of the main television and radio channels — at nearly 900 feet (270 metres) it is the tallest structure in London. A second one ahead is NTL's South Norwood transmitter. *A grand stairway leads up to the terraces, which have become a sort of wilderness, awaiting a decision on their future. A diversion is worthwhile for the view, and to search for overgrown foundations of the features that surrounded the palace.*

Keep ahead, past the main car park, along a road leading out through the park gates **AZ**, with the sports-centre entrance to your left. Cross the road and take the fenced path opposite to the left, then shortly turn right down seven steps and pass the original station building to the more recent entrance to Crystal Palace Station **BA**. *Wheelchairs can avoid the steps by going ahead from the park gates **AZ** along a pavement beside low concrete bollards, then turning left to the station.*

# 4 CRYSTAL PALACE TO STREATHAM

**Distance**: 3.9 miles (6.3 km). Excludes Capital Ring link of 0.1 miles (0.2 km) to Streatham Common Station.

**Public transport.** Walk 4 starts at the exit from Crystal Palace Station with bus stops nearby. It has a link with Streatham Station, and finishes 200 yards from Streatham Common Station and bus stops. Crystal Palace Station and Anerley Hill are in Travelcard and Bus Zone 4. Church Road, Chevening Road, Beulah Hill, Streatham and Streatham Common are in Zone 3.

**Surface and terrain.** On tarmac or paving throughout. However, walkers with dogs will have to make a diversion of 200 yards on grass at Norwood Grove. Crystal Palace to Church Road: includes a long and very steep ascent. Church Road to Beulah Hill: includes a very steep descent and a fairly steep ascent. Beulah Hill to Streatham: mostly level but with two fairly steep descents and one fairly steep ascent.

**Refreshments.** Anerley Hill, Church Road, The Rookery, Streatham.

**Toilets.** Westow Road, The Rookery, Streatham Common.

Walk 4 starts at Crystal Palace Station **A** in the London Borough of Bromley. From the station exit cross Crystal Palace Station Road then bear half-left through a small public garden to Anerley Hill **B**. Cross at the lights towards the Paxton Arms Hotel, turn right then shortly left into Pleydell Avenue, with the Crystal Palace television transmitter up to the right. You are now in one of the hilliest parts of South London and will soon be climbing steeply over two ridges.

At the end of Pleydell Avenue, bear right then left through Palace Square **C**. Keep ahead up a steep, zigzag footpath beside a playground and grass area. Ahead is Belvedere Road **D**, apparently so named after the houses it contained – *belvedere* means 'beautiful view' in Italian. Look left and you will see two such houses, with their rooftop belvederes, built in the late 19th century. Cross and turn right up Belvedere Road, noting handsome Belvedere Court opposite. Shortly turn left into Tudor Road **E**, where there are more fine old residences, especially Tudor House and Barton House. At the end, pass Lansdowne Place then turn right into Fox Hill **F**. At A212 Church Road **G** turn right, cross at the refuge and enter Westow Park **1**, where you pass into the London Borough of Croydon. You are now in the district of Norwood, which takes its name from the ancient Great North Wood (see Walk 3).

Descend the steep hill through Westow Park to a gate, where you turn left, but look up to your right to see the spire of the Greek

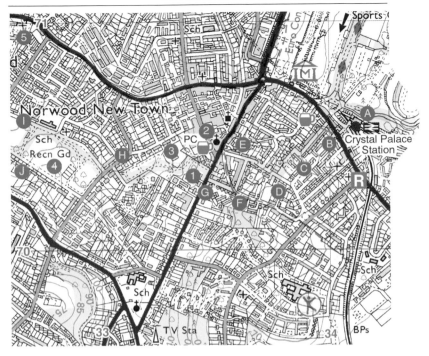

Orthodox Church of Saints Constantine and Helen **2**. *For toilets, go through the gate, turn left and up the stepped footpath between the garden centre and Safeway car park.* Continuing through the park, to your right beyond the trees is a long red-brick building, which was formerly part of the Royal Normal College for blind children and is now a training and family-support centre for Barnardo's **3**. Bear right at a fork, then left to pass a playground, and go round two sides of a grass square to reach a road (College Green). Turn right then shortly cross and turn left along Harold Road **H**, which is the centre of a conservation area containing substantial and decorative Victorian houses.

Cross and turn right along Chevening Road beside Upper Norwood Recreation Ground **4**. In 100 yards turn left into the park, then shortly turn right at the junction along a path, parallel to the road, where you pass a disused granite drinking fountain, dated 1891. Rejoin the road for a short distance, passing St Margaret's Church and Rockmount Primary School, then turn left into the park once more **I**. Go all the way across, passing a pavilion, while up to your left is the South Norwood transmitter again. On the far side, turn right along Eversley Road **J**, still beside the open space. Away to your right, two little spires mark the Church and Convent of the Faithful Virgin on Central Hill **5**. At the end,

*Biggin Wood is one of the largest remnants of the ancient Great North Wood, which once extended for 7 miles between Croydon and Deptford.*

turn left up Hermitage Road **K** to the top and A215 Beulah Hill **L**. Go over the zebra crossing, then turn right. The little house with the green tiled roof was the lodge of a mansion called Woodlands.

Along Beulah Hill, number 75 has a black plaque to indicate that from 1946 to 1973 it was the home of Joan and Alan Warwick, founders of the Norwood Society. There are many more fine residences along the left-hand side. Cross Downsview Road **M**, then in 300 yards turn left down Biggin Hill **N**, using the left-hand pavement. A short way down on your left is a modern residential development called Dickens Wood Close. The name is significant, as it occupies the site of Springfield **6**, where Charles Dickens stayed and set the scene for David Copperfield to meet Dora Spenlow. After passing some allotments, cross via a refuge to the opposite pavement, then in 50 yards, opposite number 47, turn right along a footpath **O**. This leads past tennis courts and toilets (closed at the time of writing) into Biggin Wood **7**, another remnant of the Great North Wood.

Continue ahead along a tarmac footpath to the far side of the wood. At the road, proceed to a junction **P** then bear right along Covington Way, using the right-hand pavement. Stenton Covington (1856–1935) was a very active local campaigner who did a great deal for this area. Keep ahead at the crossroads (Norbury Hill), then cross a road called Christian Fields. At Gibson's Hill **Q** turn right through a gate into a park called Norwood Grove **8**. Follow a narrow tarmac path that winds up through the park. At a fork keep ahead to reach a gate **R** in a metal fence. *Dogs are not permitted inside the enclosure; they must be taken along a signed Capital Ring diversion on grass, outside the fence.*

Dogless walkers may pass through the gate, then immediately turn left. You soon have a fine view to your right of the mansion **9**, also called Norwood Grove, and its gardens. You should also have a fine view to the left across Croydon towards the North Downs. Keep ahead beside the fence and pass through an arched rose arbour. At the terrace, turn right to go around two sides of the mansion and its orangery. Norwood Grove, the park, was once part of Streatham Common. Norwood Grove, the mansion, known locally as the White House, was originally much larger — only the east wing of the original building survives. It was built during the 1840s for Arthur Anderson, joint founder of P&O (Peninsular and Oriental Steam Navigation Company), MP for the Shetland Isles, and said to have been a keen early supporter of Crystal Palace Football Club.

At the far corner of the mansion, go through a gate **S**, where the dog diversion rejoins the main route. Turn left through another gate, then immediately left again into a drive. Bear right past a barrier and continue along the fenced drive to a lodge. Here you cross into the London Borough of Lambeth: the boundary is marked by a tiny stream

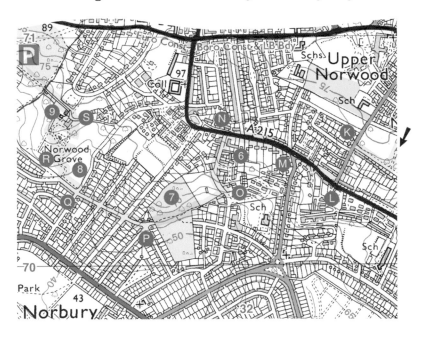

that feeds the River Graveney, itself a tributary of the Wandle, and a line of 400-year-old oak trees **10**. Continue along the drive, now on Streatham Common **11**, to reach a car park, with The Rookery gardens **12** on your left, featured in many guides to the best public gardens. South-west London is blessed with a string of extensive commons, most of which were saved from development by a variety of bodies during the 19th century. This did not, however, save them from being sliced up by roads and railways, and most now lie in several separate pieces. All these commons were once wild areas, owned by the local squire, where people from the surrounding villages had certain rights, including grazing animals and collecting firewood, berries and nuts. Four are crossed by the Capital Ring, Streatham Common being the first.

At the road (Streatham Common South) **T**, bear left to pass the Rookery café, *beside which is an automatic toilet*. Cross the road to the next part of the common, noting the old granite water trough, one of many installed around London by the Metropolitan Drinking Fountain and Cattle Trough Association. It is now a planter, but still has water at dog level. The seat nearby has a Millennium topograph set into its concrete base. Bear left down the common on a narrow tarmac footpath towards A23 Streatham High Road. The church tower ahead belongs to Streatham's Parish Church of Immanuel and

*Norwood Grove and its lovely gardens, near Streatham Common.*

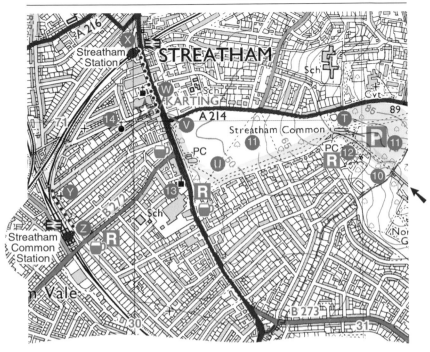

St Andrew **13**. Shortly before reaching the main road, bear half-right on a tarmac path **U**, then right again to walk parallel to the road.

You pass a playground, *behind which are more toilets*. The original Capital Ring link to Streatham Common Station along Greyhound Lane may still be signed here, but it has been superseded. At a road called Streatham Common North, cross ahead to Streatham Memorial Gardens **V**, then cross left over Streatham High Road to the junction with Lewin Road **W**. Streatham High Road is one of the longest shopping centres in London, stretching for 1 1/2 miles. The famous ice rink is just along here on the left.

**Capital Ring link to Streatham Station** *(0.2 miles / 0.3 km). Turn right along Streatham High Road to Streatham Station **X**. If starting here, from the station exit turn right along Streatham High Road for 300 yards to the junction with Lewin Road **W**, cross it and turn right along the left-hand pavement.*

Keep ahead along the left-hand side of Lewin Road. You pass the red-brick Streatham Baptist Church **14**. Walk 4 ends at the junction with Estreham Road **Y**, where you can turn left for 200 yards to Streatham Common Station **Z** or a little further for buses in Greyhound Lane. *Walk 5 continues ahead over the footbridge.*

# 5 STREATHAM TO WIMBLEDON PARK

**Distance**: 5.4 miles (8.7 km). Excludes a Capital Ring link of 0.1 miles (0.2 km) from Streatham Common Station.

**Public transport.** The start of Walk 5 is 200 yards from Streatham Common Station and bus stops. The route passes Earlsfield and Wandsworth Common Stations, and there is a link with Balham Station. The finish is at Wimbledon Park Station and 250 yards from bus stops. All places on this walk are in Travelcard and Bus Zone 3, except Trinity Road, Wandsworth, which is in Zone 2.

**Surface and terrain.** Almost all of this walk is on level paving or tarmac, with just one very short stretch of earth path. There is a stepped footbridge soon after the start (a suggested diversion is described), and a gentle ascent at the end.

**Refreshments**: Streatham, Tooting Common, Balham, Wandsworth Common, Trinity Road, Earlsfield and Wimbledon Park.

**Toilets.** Balham and Earlsfield.

*Capital Ring link from Streatham Common Station (0.1 miles / 0.2 km).*
*From the station exit A turn left through the car park and continue ahead along Estreham Road to the junction with Lewin Road. Here you join the Capital Ring, which comes along Lewin Road.*

Walk 5 starts at the junction of Lewin Road and Estreham Road **B** in the London Borough of Lambeth. Cross the footbridge (26 steps) over one of several railway lines that merge here to form Streatham Junction **1**. *You can avoid the footbridge by continuing along Estreham Road for 220 yards, then at the bend turn left through a ramped subway to Potter's Lane C, where you turn right along Conyers Road; skip the next paragraph if you follow this diversion.*

Follow the fenced footpath through a no-man's-land between and below the railway lines, with trains hurtling past in all directions. Up to your left is the main line from Victoria to the Sussex coast, opened in 1846 for the London, Brighton and South Coast Railway and popularly known as the Brighton Line. At the end, turn right into Potter's Lane **C**, where some pleasant dwellings appear to tolerate the railway mayhem, then turn left along Conyers Road.

Shortly on your left now lies an oddity: a yellow-brick Moorish temple, topped with several green copper cupolas, which is in fact Thames Water's Streatham Pumping Station **2**, built in 1888. Further on, at number 14, look out for the rather startling stained-glass window depicting a woman watching a departing sailing ship. At the

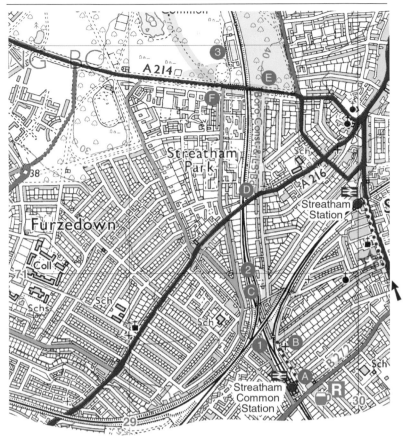

end of Conyers Road cross A216 Mitcham Lane **D** — if the road is busy, use the refuge to the right — and keep ahead along tree-lined Riggindale Road. On your right is Streatham Methodist Church, built in 1900, which has a very wide, barrel-vaulted ceiling. At the end of the road, bear left on a footpath up a bank leading to A214 Tooting Bec Road **E**, with Tooting Common Woodlands opposite.

Turn left over the railway, entering as you do so the London Borough of Wandsworth, and cross at the traffic lights **F**. Turn left on the far side, past the approach to Tooting Bec Lido **3**. Opened in 1906, it is one of the largest swimming pools in Europe at 100 yards long and 33 yards wide. In 1936, following the fashion of the day, it was rebuilt in 'lido' style, taking this name from a fashionable bathing beach near Venice, with a large open-air pool and a paddling pool surrounded by extensive sunbathing areas.

Immediately bear half-right along a tarmac footpath onto the southern part of Tooting Bec Common **4**. The name Bec comes from the granting of this parish to the abbey of St Mary de Bec in Normandy during the 12th century. There are actually two Tooting Commons, Graveney and Bec; the Capital Ring crosses the latter. Halfway across, behind a copse, lies a lake — said to contain terrapins, though this is almost certainly an urban myth. The park café lies off to the left a little further on. At the road, Bedford Hill **G**, named after the Duke of Bedford who used to own much of this area, cross at the refuge and continue ahead across the northern part of the common. Soon you bear left, between houses to your left and the Brighton Line again to your right. In 80 yards turn left by a notice board **H** along a short, fenced footpath.

Cross Culverden Road and go ahead along Fontenoy Road. Back at Bedford Hill **I**, turn right to cross at the refuge, then turn right and immediately left into Ritherdon Road, following the left-hand pavement. Pass Carminia and Childebert Roads, then cross over and turn right along Cloudesdale Road **J**, using the right-hand pavement. At the end, cross and turn left along Elmfield Road **K**, passing Balham

*The Capital Ring crosses Tooting Bec Common close to its 'terrapin pond'.*

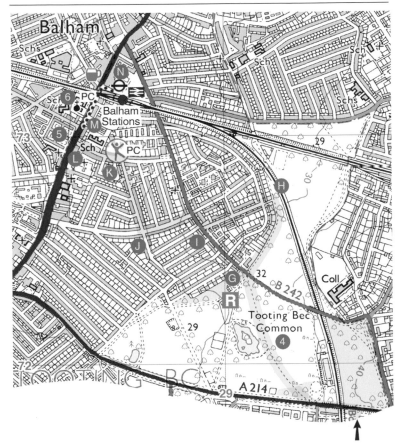

Leisure Centre, *which has toilets*. Pass Ravenstone School to reach Balham High Road **L**, opposite Du Cane Court **5**. Despite its rather bland exterior, Du Cane Court is one of the most elegant apartment blocks in South London, dating from the Art Deco period of the 1930s. Turn right to the traffic lights **M**.

**Capital Ring link with Balham Station** *(0.1 miles / 0.2 km). Keep ahead past the traffic lights to the railway bridge, where there is an automatic toilet. Balham railway and London Underground stations **N** are on the right past the bridge. If starting here, from the station exits go under the railway bridge for 200 yards to the traffic lights **M**.*

Cross Balham High Road at the traffic lights. Nearby is Balham's parish church of St Mary and John the Divine **6**, dating from 1808. Projecting in front is an unusual domed baptistry, and the original bell still chimes the hours and announces services. Turn left and immediately

*One of the ponds on Wandsworth Common has a boardwalk, which provides an excellent viewpoint into the aquatic habitats.*

right along Balham Park Road, then in 200 yards cross Boundaries Road **O** and continue ahead. At the bend, turn right along a passage **P** onto Wandsworth Common **7**, which is quite extensive but has been shattered by roads and railway into several shards. For a third time you encounter the Brighton Line, passing impertinently through the ticket office of Wandsworth Common Station **Q**. Follow the station approach road round to the left and cross at the lights over both St James's Drive and Bellevue Road, passing the Hope pub **R**. Take the furthest right of three paths onto the next part of Wandsworth Common, rejoining the railway line. You pass three ponds: the third has a boardwalk and viewing platform.

At the footbridge **S** over the railway, keep ahead then straight-away fork left on the third path, heading for the right-hand end of a long brick wall. The green and cream building to your right, the former Neal's Farmhouse **8**, now contains park offices and a nature study centre run by the London Borough of Wandsworth. Those with energy to spare could try the trim trail that leads off to your left, on a circuit that brings you back to the footbridge. To continue, bear left between the fences then keep ahead, parallel to Dorlcote Road. Towards the end, bear left up a short earth path to the traffic lights at Trinity Road **T**. Cross at the lights and continue ahead beside the County Arms pub along Alma Terrace. Ahead loom the forbidding brick wall and buildings of Wandsworth Prison **9**, built in 1851 as the Surrey House of Correction. Former inmates include Oscar Wilde in 1895, imprisoned for homosexuality (you shortly pass a street called Wilde Place), and in 1963 the Great Train Robber Ronnie Biggs, until his notorious escape in 1965. In 1953, Derek Bentley was hanged here, wrongfully convicted of the murder of a policeman; the conviction was overturned in 1998.

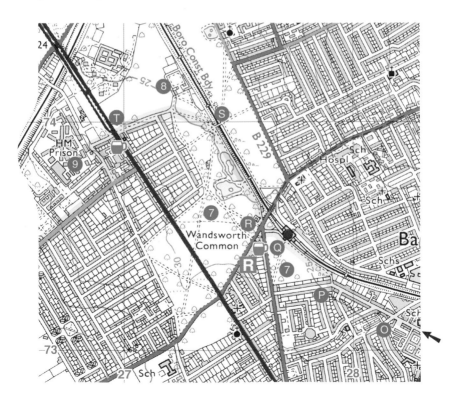

Turn left beside the prison along Heathfield Road **U**. At the mini-roundabout **V**, turn right into the long and straight Magdalen Road, which you follow for half a mile. On your left, opposite Magdalen Park Bowling and Tennis Clubs, note Slane House with its *belvedere*. Most of this road adjoins Wandsworth Cemetery **10**, which is open to the public, and you can if you prefer walk the length of the cemetery by entering at the main gate **W** and following the parallel path to leave by a swing gate **X** at the far end. *Towards the end of Magdalen Road, beside Earlsfield Public Library, is an automatic toilet.* At A217 Garratt Lane **Y**, turn right past Earlsfield Station **Z** and under the railway bridge to the junction with Earlsfield Road **AA**, then cross left at the lights and keep ahead along Penwith Road.

You shortly cross the River Wandle **11**, which flows through Mitcham to join the Thames at Wandsworth. It was once one of the fastest-flowing rivers in the London area, providing some of the best trout fishing in Britain and power for a host of watermills. This used to be one of London's most active industrial areas, and it must have been a nauseous place. Soap and chemical manure were produced nearby, while a fireworks factory consisted of wooden huts, set some distance apart so that an explosion in one was less likely to ignite another. The decline of industrial activity in recent years has allowed much of the Wandle to be turned into a nature reserve. This is more evident further south, but only a few hundred yards away to the left, at Trewint Street, a narrow band of greenery stretches almost unbroken for nearly 2 miles to Colliers Wood. The Wandle Trail, which you cross at Garratt Lane, accompanies the river for 11 miles from Waddon to Wandsworth.

Shortly turn left into Ravensbury Terrace **AB**, then bear right with the bend, passing the Haslemere Industrial Estate, into Haslemere Avenue **AC**, where you enter the London Borough of Merton. Cross Dawlish Avenue and Brooklands Avenue, keeping ahead into Mount Road. Take the next left, Lucien Road **AD**, and go through the gate **AE** at the end into Durnsford Road Recreation Ground **12**. Follow the tarmac path round to the right, past a school and playground, into Wellington Road **AF**. Turn left, then at the end, beside Field Court **AG**, turn right along a short footpath leading to Durnsford Road **AH**.

Turn left to cross at the lights, towards the white-tiled, minaretted Wimbledon Mosque **13**, opened in 1977. Turn left along the far side for 150 yards, then turn right up Arthur Road **AI**. In 250 yards you cross at the lights for Wimbledon Park Station **AJ**, where Walk 5 finishes. *To continue on to Walk 6, stay on the right-hand side and keep ahead.* Buses serve Durnsford Road just before the finish, near the junction with Arthur Road **AI**.

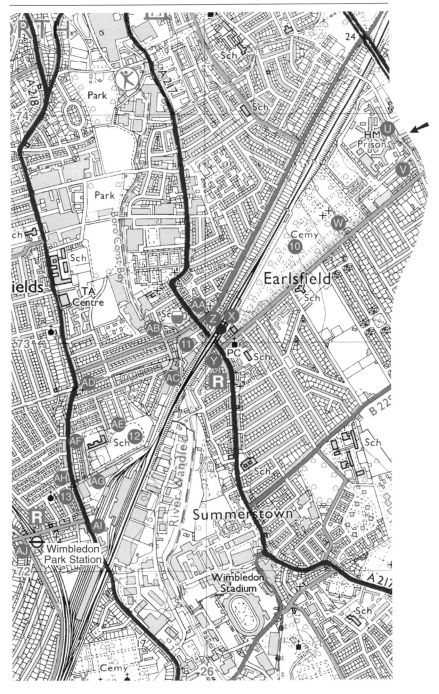

# 6 WIMBLEDON PARK TO RICHMOND

**Distance**: 6.9 miles (11.2 km). Excludes link of 0.5 miles (0.8 km) to Richmond Station.

**Public transport**. Walk 5 starts at Wimbledon Park Station, with buses 250 yards away in Durnsford Road. It finishes near Richmond Bridge, which has buses nearby and is half a mile from Richmond Station. Wimbledon Park and Wimbledon Park Side are in Travelcard and Bus Zone 3; Kingston Vale, Petersham and Richmond are in Zone 4.

**Surface and terrain**. The first 2 miles are on pavements or tarmac paths — level at first, then a fairly steep climb up to Putney Heath. Then the route is almost entirely on earth paths and tracks with some steep gradients nearly all the way to Richmond. The final stretch beside the Thames is on level tarmac.

**Refreshments**: Wimbledon Park, Wimbledon Common, Kingston Vale, Pembroke Lodge, Petersham and Richmond.

**Toilets**: Wimbledon Park, Wimbledon Common and Richmond Park.

**Signs**. Note that street signs in Kingston and Richmond boroughs have a black background instead of the standard green, to meet local planning requirements.

Walk 6 starts in Arthur Road, SW19 opposite Wimbledon Park Station **A**, in the London Borough of Merton. *From the station exit, turn left along Arthur Road, using the width restrictor to cross to the far side.* Shortly turn right along Home Park Road, then in 200 yards turn right through a gate **B** into Wimbledon Park **1**, one of London's oldest recreational open spaces. It was formed towards the end of the 16th century from part of Wimbledon Common, and originally included the golf course and what is now the All England Lawn Tennis and Croquet Club. The supreme landscape designer Capability Brown redesigned the park in the mid-18th century, creating the lake.

Descend several flights totalling 35 steps, passing through a viewing platform, or there is ramped access to the right. At the bottom, turn left through a gate, then follow a tarmac path through a play area, keeping to the edge of the trees. *Over to your right, by tennis courts, are toilets and a seasonal, chalet-style café.* Fork left at a climbing frame and leave the play area through another gate, then take the path up to Wimbledon Park Lake **2**. Note the twisted-wire sculpture offshore — a popular bird perch. You should see plenty of waterbirds and maybe some sailing boats. The spire of Wimbledon's

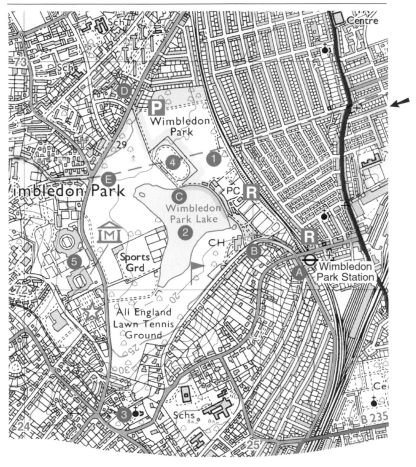

parish church of St Mary **3** is prominent on the hill beyond. Follow the lakeside path to its end, past the sailing base. At a fence by gates **C**, turn right to go around three sides of the athletics stadium **4**, the home of Hercules Wimbledon Athletic Club. At the gates on the far side of the stadium, turn right to the park exit **D**.

Go out into Wimbledon Park Road and turn left beside the park, entering the London Borough of Wandsworth. To your left, across Wimbledon Park Golf Course, is another view of the lake. For the next couple of miles you follow the boundary between Merton (to your left) and Wandsworth (to your right), switching back and forth between the two boroughs. In 350 yards you reach a mini-round-about **E**. Ahead now and on the right is the All England Lawn Tennis and Croquet Club **5** with its tennis museum — this area is heaving with

*Wimbledon Park's lake, created by Capability Brown, is enlivened by sailing dinghie*

*nd water birds. Beyond the poplars lies the park's athletics stadium.*

*Wimbledon Common's unusual 19th-century hollow post mill rises above a museum devoted to windmills.*

activity during Wimbledon fortnight at the end of June and beginning of July. Immediately after the roundabout, turn right across the road at a refuge, then keep ahead along Bathgate Road. In 175 yards, turn right into Queensmere Road **F**. To your left lies the impressive Royal Close **6**, now converted into luxury apartments. It used to be Queensmere House, formerly a college, which was a prisoner-of-war camp for officers during World War II. You climb fairly steeply for 700 yards, eventually reaching A219 Wimbledon Park Side **G**.

Turn right and cross at the traffic lights **H** onto wooded Putney Heath **7**. Fork left, then keep ahead to a broad gravel track bearing left. Nearly all of the remainder of Walk 6 is on such tracks and paths, and may be muddy in places. The logo on signposts here shows that you are sharing this track with the Windmill Nature Trail. At the end, you reach an open area near the famous windmill **8**. Cross a broad track and keep ahead on a path, which bears left at the end towards the mill, beside which are a museum and tearoom. The windmill, built in 1817, is most unusual, being the only remaining example in Britain of a hollow post mill: the main body of the mill, with all its machinery, originally turned on a central post, through which a hole was bored for a drive shaft taking power to the machinery. This was replaced in 1893 by an iron bearing. Putney Heath and Wimbledon Common together form one of the largest public open spaces in Greater London. The route of the Capital Ring lies mostly on Putney Heath, peeping into Wimbledon Common **9** in the area around the windmill.

Keep ahead on a dirt path **I** between the tearoom and car park, passing toilets. Bear left past the clubhouse of the London Scottish Golf Club, whose red-lion coat of arms adorns the gables. You can easily identify its members, who are required to wear red tops while playing. At the end of the hedge and fence, just before the golf course, turn right down a broad earth path, which descends fairly steeply for 250 yards to Queen's Mere **10**, formed in 1887 by damming a stream that feeds Beverley Brook. In Elizabeth Beresford's books, this was a favourite retreat of the Wombles, although its serene appearance is rather disturbed by the distant roar of the A3.

At the narrow end of the mere **J**, bear left up a clear rising track amid trees. At the top you must cross a golf fairway; watch out for

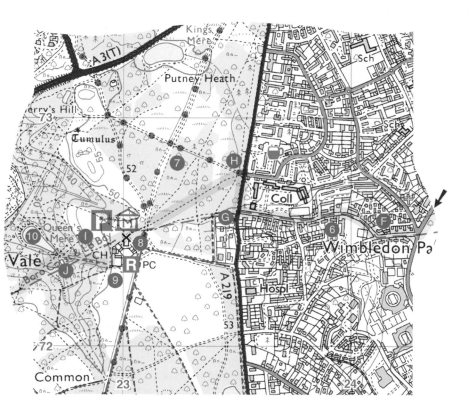

rapidly approaching golf balls. Bear half-right to continue along the track through more trees, then cross a second fairway; again, take care. Back amid the trees, take the middle track of three **K**, with a bench seat on your right, and follow it for 175 yards down to a track junction. Continue downhill to the next junction **L**. Ahead now, through the trees, are the circular, hedge-bound Memorial Gardens **11**, with a World War I memorial at its centre. Turn left along a broad and usually muddy track as it swings right. At a grassy triangle **M**, bear right on a narrow footpath, which soon joins tracks beside Beverley Brook **12**. Bear right, with the brook just to your left, to pass a wooden footbridge. The brook rises in Nonsuch Park near Cheam and flows through New Malden and Richmond Park to the Thames at Putney. For the next half-mile the Capital Ring joins the Beverley Brook Walk, marked by its cerise and yellow waymarks. To your right now is the training ground of Wimbledon Football Club.

In 350 yards turn left to cross a brick-walled footbridge **N** over the brook, with the training-ground pavilion to your right (its well-marked toilets are not for public use). For the next 500 yards, the Capital Ring pays a very brief visit to the Royal Borough of Kingston-upon-Thames. Take the right fork, then bear half-left on a narrow path across grass, heading for the footbridge **O** over the A3 Kingston Bypass (Robin Hood Way). Cross first the high footbridge over the A3, with widely spaced steps, then a controlled crossing over A308 Kingston Vale. Turn right along the far side, then in 70 yards turn left, before the late-18th-century

*According to Elizabeth Beresford, Queen's Mere is a spot favoured by the Wombles.*

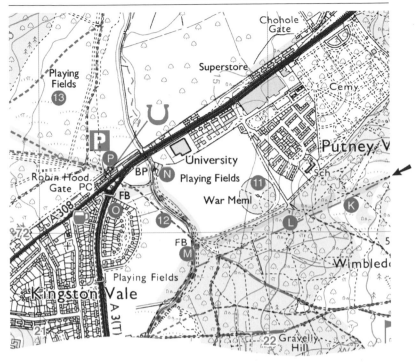

Stag Lodge Stables, and go through Robin Hood Gate **P** into Richmond Park **13**. *There are toilets on your left inside the gate.* The rest of Walk 6 lies in the London Borough of Richmond-upon-Thames. For centuries, Richmond Park was used by England's hunting-mad royalty, and in 1637 was enclosed for their sole use by Charles I. The park is still owned by the Crown and managed by the Royal Parks Agency. It is now a national nature reserve and the largest urban park in Europe at around 2$^1/_2$ miles from side to side and top to bottom. Towards the centre, the view as far as you can see consists of woods, meadows and ponds. Richmond Park is famous for its deer, of which the park has around 650. There are two kinds: red (the darker, larger ones) and fallow (the smaller, light-brown, dappled ones). It is worth quoting the park's warning notices: 'It is always dangerous to go close to the deer, but especially in May, June, July and October. Feeding or touching the deer is prohibited. Dogs must be kept under control and not be allowed to worry the deer. Dogs approaching too closely may be attacked.'

The roads inside Richmond Park are heavily used by traffic, so take care as you cross the road and go through the car park to its entrance. Cross another road, then keep ahead on a well-worn path through grass and among widely spaced trees into a wide, open pasture.

*The Pen Ponds in Richmond Park, a haven for water birds, were created by damming a stream that feeds Beverley Brook.*

Follow the path as it climbs steadily, heading for the left end of Spankers Hill Wood. You cross the brow of the hill to find a car park **Q** ahead, with a seasonal refreshment kiosk, although at the time of writing there was a proposal to close this car park.

Keep ahead along a track towards the distant Pen Ponds. Away to the right among trees is White Lodge **14**, built around 1727 and now the home of the Royal Ballet School. Further on comes an area of tussock grass, where the park management is encouraging the ground nesting of birds such as skylarks, reed bunting, stonechat and meadow pipit — dogs should be kept on a lead here. You pass between the Pen Ponds **15** on a gravel path, usually lined with family groups observing the antics of water birds. These ponds, too, were formed by damming a stream that feeds Beverley Brook. If it feels especially cold here on a winter's day, blame it on the topography: the Pen Ponds lie in a notorious frost hollow.

This is a very peaceful area, though you may hear distant traffic on the park roads, and you are directly beneath a flight path to Heathrow Airport. Once past the ponds, keep going in the same direction, climbing a track through more tussock grass. Halfway up, you cross a broad track, with a lightning-blasted tree on your right, then in a further 100 yards, shortly before a second blasted tree at the brow, turn left along a level path **R**.

You come now to Sidmouth Wood **16**, named after Lord Sidmouth, who was responsible for planting most of the park's woodlands during the early 19th century. Follow the track by the fence **S** ahead. Except when trees are in full leaf, away to the left soon you should see Whiteash Pond and Whiteash Lodge, built in the mid-18th century and now a base for the Royal Parks Constabulary. As the track

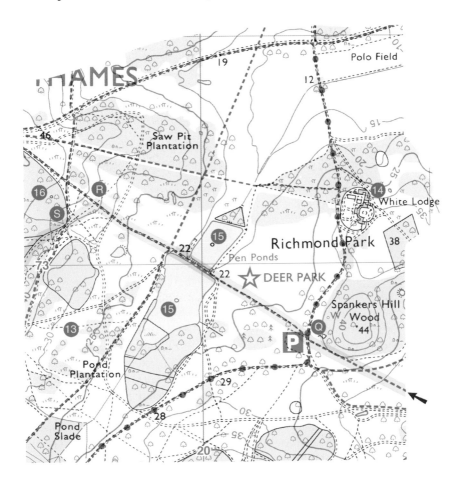

swings right, you pass Oak Lodge **17**, built in 1850 and now accommodating some of the park's management staff. Follow its tarmac drive ahead to the western park road **T**.

Cross the road carefully and keep ahead along an earth path for 75 yards, passing a gate **U** into Pembroke Lodge Gardens — use this entrance into the cafeteria if you wish to avoid the steep steps later. Go down the slope and bear right, with a great view to your left. You are now in Petersham Park **18**, added to Richmond Park in 1843. It contains some beautiful trees, and deer can be seen here too. Follow the path parallel to the fence, passing another gate **V** into the gardens. Pembroke Lodge **19** is close by up a steep flight of steps. Originally the home of the park's molecatcher, in 1788 it was converted into an imposing residence for the Countess of Pembroke. During the 19th and early 20th centuries it was occupied by various members of the aristocratic Russell family, and philosopher Bertrand spent his childhood here. Requisitioned for military use during World War II, it subsequently became the park's rather grand cafeteria.

In a further 250 yards at a bench **W**, the Capital Ring bears half-left downhill, *but a short diversion is recommended to the right to see the King Henry VIII Mound* **20**, *reached through another gate into the gardens*. The mound is actually a prehistoric round barrow or burial mound, but has

*Richmond Bridge has spanned the Thames for more than two centuries.*

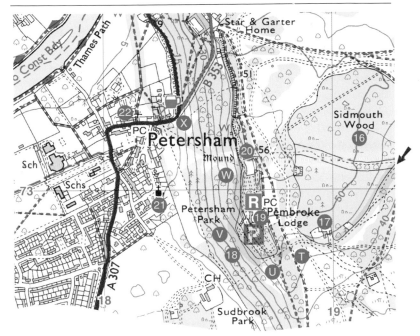

a sinister connection with Henry. He is supposed to have stood here in 1536, looking out for a flare from the Tower of London which would confirm that Anne Boleyn had been executed, leaving him free to marry Lady Jane Seymour. The view is extensive, to the hills of Berkshire and Surrey.

As you descend towards Petersham village, the view across West London is dominated by the massive stands of 'Twickers' — Twickenham Rugby Ground. The eye-catching, romanesque red-brick building to your left, with campanile, is All Saints' Church **21**. It was built in 1908 as a second church for Petersham, which at that time was expected to grow larger than it did. Currently closed, this attractive but rather sad church has lain unused for most of its history, and its future seems uncertain, though there was a proposal to turn it into a luxury home. The little white bell tower ahead, with wind vane, sits on top of Petersham's much older parish church of St Peter **22**, dating from the 13th century. You leave the park through Petersham Gate **X**; *there are toilets in the playground to your left*. The gate occupies a gap in the 8-mile-long, 8-feet-high brick wall that almost completely surrounds Richmond Park and its adjoining territories. Local brickmakers must have made a killing out of this project in 1637 when the park was enclosed — by the author's estimate, over five million bricks would have been needed.

You must now cross the A307 Petersham Road, but as it is usually very busy you are advised to cross at traffic lights 70 yards to the right. The route continues opposite, beside Café Dysart, along a fenced earth footpath, which twists and turns between sheds and St Peter's churchyard. Turn right along a driveway. *If you wish to visit the church, turn left. Hidden away in the churchyard, by the south wall, is the tomb of the 18th-century explorer Captain George Vancouver, a Petersham resident.*

At a bend **Y** in the drive, keep ahead along a footpath through Petersham Meadows **23**. Famously painted by Turner, and usually occupied by cattle, these fields are regularly flooded by the Thames with permission, as it were, from the local authority — this helps to maintain them in their natural state. Up to your right is the imposing Royal Star and Garter Home **24**, a retirement home for disabled ex-servicemen and women, established in 1916. Keep ahead at a barrier **Z**, gradually closing in on the riverside. Go through a swing gate and keep ahead through Buccleuch Gardens **AA**, *with toilets on your right.*

For the next 3 miles, the Capital Ring shares the route of the Thames Path National Trail, one of 13 such routes in England and Wales. Launched in 1996, it runs for 184 miles (295 km) from the source of the river near Cirencester in Gloucestershire, through Oxford, Reading, Windsor and central London to finish at the Thames Barrier. The Thames itself is 205 miles (330 km) in length, continuing to The Nore sandbank, between Southend and Sheerness, where it formally ceases to be an estuary and becomes open sea. Follow the broad, tarmac path beside the river, with the handsome Richmond Bridge **25** ahead, opened in 1777. You pass three low stone arches, which used to form the entrance to a subway under the road into Terrace Gardens, though this has recently been closed. Boathouses, refreshment kiosks and some rather smart eating establishments line the path. To your right lies the bustling town of Richmond **26**, named by King Henry VII after his estate in Yorkshire when he built his new palace here. At that time, it was just a small fishing village, which until then had been called Shene.

At Richmond Bridge **AB**, keep ahead along Richmond Riverside **27**, one of the most impressive stretches beside the Thames. Its terraced gardens and adjacent buildings, dating from the 17th and 19th centuries and previously rather dilapidated, were beautifully restored in the 1980s. The grey stone building ahead, now a wine bar, was originally the Waterworks Pump House and later served as a brewery. There are several small islands in the river here, the largest being Corporation Island. *For toilets, climb the steps to the right past the 'Pro Patria' war memorial and keep ahead a short distance along Whittaker Avenue, where the facilities are to be found outside the Old Town Hall.* Pass the old White Cross pub at the foot of Water Lane **AC**, then St Helena Pier — this area may be under water at high tide. Soon after this, Walk 6 ends at Friars Lane **AD**. *Walk 7 continues ahead; or for its alternative route, avoiding the steps at Richmond Lock, turn right up Friars Lane, then turn right at the top into King Street (see Walk 7).*

***Capital Ring link to Richmond Station*** *(0.5 mile / 0.8 km). Turn right up Friars Lane, using the pavement on the right-hand side, angling around a car park. At the top, keep ahead across two roads, watching out for traffic from the right. Keep ahead along a gravel path across Richmond Green* **AE***. At the end cross right then left across Duke Street* **AF** *and keep ahead along Little Green, passing Richmond Theatre. Continue over the railway bridge then immediately turn right up an alleyway* **AG** *to a road called The Quadrant. Turn right to cross at the lights, then turn left to Richmond Station* **AH***.*

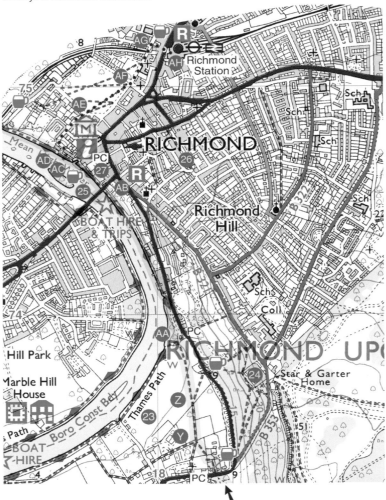

# 7 RICHMOND TO OSTERLEY LOCK

**Distance**: 3.8 miles (6.1 km). Excludes Capital Ring links 0.5 miles (0.8 km) from Richmond Station and 0.5 miles (0.8 km) to Boston Manor Station.

**Public transport**. The start of Walk 7 is near Richmond Bridge, close to bus stops. Richmond Station is half a mile away. There is a link en route with Brentford Station. The finish at Osterley Lock is 500 yards from bus stops and half a mile from Boston Manor Station. All places on Walk 7 are in Travelcard and Bus Zone 4.

**Surface and terrain**. Entirely on paving, tarmac or bonded gravel, except for a 600-yard stretch on grass in Syon Park with a parallel tarmac drive. Mostly level, but there are some short and fairly steep ascents along the Grand Union Canal towpath. There is a stepped footbridge over the Thames at Richmond Lock, which can be avoided on a Capital Ring alternative route. The Thames towpath north of Richmond is subject to flooding after heavy rain or at high tide. The link to Boston Manor Station includes a fairly long and steady ascent on a gravel track.

**Refreshments**: Richmond, Old Isleworth, Syon Park, Brentford and Boston Manor.

**Toilets**: Richmond and Syon Park.

**Signs**. Note that Capital Ring street signs in the London Borough of Richmond-upon-Thames have a black background instead of the standard green, to meet local planning requirements.

*Capital Ring link from Richmond Station (0.5 miles / 0.8 km). From the station's main exit **A**, turn left then cross the road (The Quadrant) at the zebra crossing. Turn right, then immediately left along a short alleyway underneath a building. Turn left over the railway, then walk along the left-hand pavement beside Little Green, passing Richmond Theatre. Cross Duke Street ahead, then immediately turn right across the road onto Richmond Green. Take the first gravel path, quarter-left, between the trees, aiming to the left of a little hut on the far side of the green. On the far side of the green **B**, cross the road and continue in the same direction along the left-hand pavement of Friars Lane. A Capital Ring alternative route starts here, avoiding the 36 steps at Richmond Lock – see next paragraph. To reach the main route, continue down Friars Lane, using the left-hand pavement, twisting left then right past a car park to the River Thames **C**. You join the Capital Ring by turning right beside the river; skip the next paragraph.*

*The alternative route to avoid steps at Richmond Lock adds about 400 yards to the distance. On leaving Richmond Green **B**, instead of going down Friars Lane, turn left along King Street. At the end turn right along George Street, continuing at the traffic lights into Hill Street, then in 175 yards turn right down Bridge Street to cross Richmond Bridge **D** over the Thames. On the far side, turn right along Willoughby Road **E**, later Ducks Walk, keeping ahead along a series of paved footpaths, shared with cyclists, for*

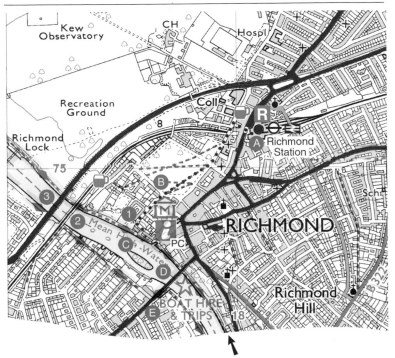

*almost half a mile parallel with the Thames. At Richmond Railway Bridge **2** you rejoin the river, then keep ahead under Twickenham Bridge **3** into Ranelagh Drive. At the footbridge over Richmond Lock and Weir **F** keep ahead, joining the Capital Ring main route; skip the next two paragraphs if you follow this diversion.*

Walk **7** of the Capital Ring starts beside the River Thames at the foot of Friars Lane **C** in the London Borough of Richmond-upon-Thames. Still in company with the Thames Path National Trail (see Walk 6), which now occupies both banks of the river for most of its journey through London, you follow the towpath for the first half-mile. Continue along the riverside, here called Cholmondeley Walk, where the gardens to your right mark the site of the great Palace of Richmond **1**. Rebuilt in 1509 by Henry VII after a fire, this was the favourite residence of Elizabeth I, who died here. After the Tudor period, the palace fell out of favour and was partially destroyed by Cromwell's troops and left to crumble. Very little of the structure remains, but three impressive later buildings occupy the grounds. Queensberry House lies back a little, as does Trumpeter's House with its impressive portico, now converted into rather grand apartments, on the site of the Middle Gate of the palace. Then, adjoining the towpath, comes the smaller Asgill House, in Palladian villa style, on the site of the palace brewhouse.

*Trumpeter's House occupies the site of the Middle Gate of Richmond Palace.*

Pass under Richmond Railway Bridge **2**, built in 1848 for the commuter line to Twickenham and Staines, then Twickenham Bridge **3** of 1933, carrying the A316 Great Chertsey Road. Ahead now are Richmond Lock and Weir, which you will shortly cross, while to your right is Old Deer Park **4**. This is part of the vast royal estate that once surrounded the Palace of Richmond, and included what is now Kew Gardens. Old Deer Park remains Crown property, but is nowadays shared between a public open space and a private sports ground. Prior to being shifted to Greenwich, the original meridian line passed through Kew Observatory, visible in the distance, which was built in 1769 for King George III. You can look along the meridian line to the observatory by squinting through a slotted metal post beside the towpath. Richmond Lock and its accompanying weir and pretty cast-iron footbridge form a neat little operation that is rather pleasing to the eye, especially when river boats are passing through. Opened in 1894, it is actually a half-tide lock, by which boats can pass over the weir two hours either side of high tide. Climb the 36 steps up to the footbridge over Richmond Lock and Weir **5**. On the far side **F**, descend steps to the right, as the alternative route comes in from the left.

Keep beside the riverside along Ranelagh Drive to a board describing the River Crane Walk, which finishes here after accompanying that river from Feltham. Continue along the riverside footpath, which leads to gardens. Behind the brick wall here is the red-brick Gordon House, with its clocktower, now part of the Twickenham Campus of Brunel University **6**. Gordon House dates from the 17th century. In

1897, it became the Industrial School for Girls, and later the Maria Gray Teacher Training College. This was absorbed into the West London Institute of Higher Education, which was itself taken over in 1995 by Brunel University, whose main base is at Uxbridge.

You reach the end of Railshead Road **G**, which used to serve a ferry. Beyond the houseboat mooring ahead lies Isleworth Ait **9** (see below) and an inaccessible stretch of river bank. It is hoped that a new riverside section will be available here soon, but for the moment you must divert left along the road for a short distance to A3004 Richmond Road in St Margaret's. Turn right to cross the River Crane **7** and enter the London Borough of Hounslow, where the Capital Ring signs return to their standard green background. Rising as Yeading Brook near Harrow, the Crane describes a great semicircle past Hillingdon and Heathrow Airport to reach the Thames here at St Margaret's.

Continue along Richmond Road for 400 yards, beside the wall of Nazareth House **8**, a convent and care centre. At the junction with South Street in Old Isleworth, with a mini-roundabout **H**, turn right along Lion Wharf Road. You rejoin the river beside Isleworth Ait **9**. Ait is a southern dialect word for island. The island, a designated nature reserve, has a somewhat mysterious air, being so close and densely wooded, yet inaccessible.

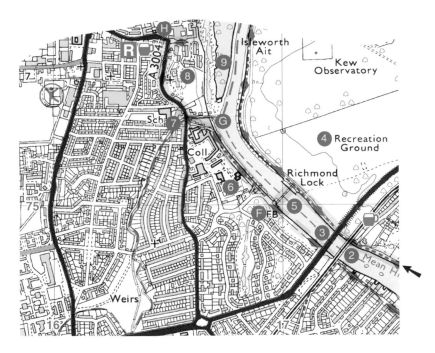

*There are many houseboat moorings along the River Thames, such as this one*

*Railshead opposite Isleworth Ait.*

Turn left beside the river at the Town Wharf pub **I** and climb onto its veranda. You may have to thread your way between customers' chairs, but do not feel intimidated or obliged to stop for a drink, as this is a public right of way. Cross a humped wooden footbridge, then at the 'electric pedestal crane' bear left to cross a bridge over the mouth of the Duke of Northumberland's River **10**. Often abbreviated to Duke's River, this is an artificial channel of uncertain age, possibly dating from the 15th century, and links the Rivers Colne and Thames. It was originally known as the Isleworth Mill Stream, providing water power, and received its current name when acquired by the Duke of Northumberland in 1605.

Another short inaccessible stretch of Thames river bank lies ahead. Follow the Duke's River for a few yards then turn right under the apartment building. Turn left through the left-hand gate, then turn right along Church Street **J**, using the left-hand pavement. Number 43 on the left is Richard Reynolds House, named after a 16th-century chaplain of Syon Monastery. You rejoin the riverside by the London Apprentice pub **11** and continue along the raised pavement beside All Saints **12**, the parish church of Isleworth. Isleworth lies in a very favourable riverside situation, a settlement since prehistoric times. The present All Saints Church was rebuilt in 1970 onto a 14th-century tower, after the 18th-century building was destroyed during World War II — not by enemy action but by vandals lighting a fire. The London Apprentice pub was so called because members of the City Livery Companies rowed here to celebrate completion of their apprenticeships. Peeping through the trees ahead is a pastel-pink building with a shallow green dome: this is The Pavilion, built at the start of the 19th century as a boathouse and picnic lodge for Syon Park. It lies next to The Ferry House, from which a ferry operated to the south bank for 400 years from Henry VIII's time until the start of World War II.

Continue past the graveyard and round the bend until you are opposite the gates **K** of Syon Park **13**, where you can cross the road carefully with maximum visibility for traffic in both directions. Go through the gates to follow a path on grass, to the right of and parallel to the drive. If you have to use the drive, which may be busy with traffic, walk in single file and keep right to face oncoming vehicles. Away to your left is a long lake **14**, which contains a trout fishery. Ahead, at either end of a ha-ha, lie twin lodges framing Syon House **15**. The Syon House and Park that you see today were created during the mid-18th century by the dream team of architect Robert Adam and landscape designer Capability Brown. The house is the London home of the Dukes of Northumberland, and is built on the site of a

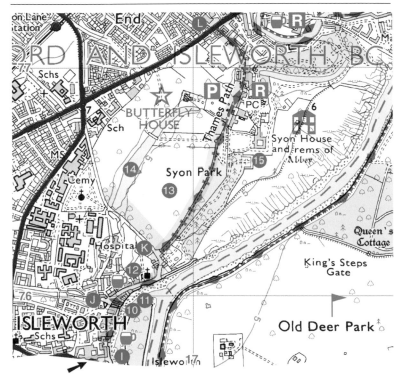

convent, which was dissolved in 1539 during Henry VIII's purge. The nuns took the name from Mount Zion, overlooking Jerusalem. When Henry died in 1547, his coffin rested at Syon en route from London to Windsor — it is said that, in divine retribution, the coffin burst open and some of his body was eaten by dogs.

The eastern part of Syon Park is now a day-out venue, offering a variety of family-oriented attractions. Continuing along the drive, you pass the garden centre, needlecraft centre, pet-care centre, butterfly house, aquatic exhibition, rose garden and children's indoor adventure playground. There is a National Trust shop, and a café and toilets are located at the entrance to Syon Park Gardens. Leave the park through Brent Lea Gate, continue to the A315 London Road **L**, then turn right to the pedestrian crossing. *For the facilities of Brentford town centre keep ahead along this side.* Archaeological evidence indicates that Brentford was probably an important trading centre in prehistoric times, because of its location, obviously, by a ford over the River Brent, as well as one over the Thames. Here you part company with the Thames Path National Trail, which turns right beside the River Brent. To continue along the Capital Ring, cross at the lights then turn right along the far side.

The Capital Ring now shares its route for several miles with the Grand Union Canal Walk and the Brent River Park Walk. Cross Commerce Road **M**, then go down the steps or past the barrier to bear left beside the Grand Union Canal. Much of this part of the canal uses the River Brent, but in places they are separate, as here, and you see the river coming in ahead, while the canal goes off through twin locks to the left. Pass the locks and go through a swing gate onto a rather bouncy swing bridge. With the ultra-modern GSK House rising ahead, you walk beside Brentford Canal Basin **16**, which is lined with warehouses that have lain derelict since the 1980s. This area is due to be redeveloped soon into a fashionable waterside district, with apartments, restaurants and a piazza. Some of the warehouses had canopies to provide shelter while loading and unloading goods, and you walk under one that survives, beside a little dock. There is a rather haunted atmosphere here, and you can imagine the ghosts of narrowboats and their crews, unloading cargo into the warehouse through its massive doors. The river and canal merge here for a while.

Pass under the railway line and continue to a second bridge **N**, which carries the A4 Great West Road through a hotbed of multinational companies. GSK House **17** is the worldwide headquarters of GlaxoSmithKline, one of the world's leading pharmaceutical and healthcare companies. It consists of four buildings linked by an enclosed 'street' with shops and restaurants for its 3000 staff.

*Capital Ring link with Brentford Station (0.4 miles / 0.7 km). At the Great West Road N, climb the steps before the bridge then turn right along the road. (There is also a ramped access point 150 yards further along the towpath, past a wooden footbridge, after which you come back along Transport Avenue and turn left along the Great West Road.) At the traffic lights, cross over, then turn right along Boston Manor Road O to Brentford Station P. If starting here, climb the steps to Boston Manor Road, turn right to the Great West Road O then turn left along it for 300 yards. Cross the canal bridge N, then descend the steps on the far side and turn left along the towpath.*

Keep ahead under the bridge. The multi-coloured steel sculpture beside GSK House opposite, entitled *Athlete*, is by Allen Jones. An added feature for towpath walkers is the dramatic reflection of the skyscape in the sheer glass walls beyond. Further on, a wooden footbridge leads to Boston Manor Park and House. The M4 now approaches noisily, high up from the right, to follow the canal for a while, as canal and river briefly split again. Yet, despite all the commercial activity in this area, the immediate surroundings of the canal are predominantly green, and you might see a roosting grey heron or two. Continue past lonely Clitherow Lock **18**, named after the family that occupied the nearby Boston Manor House for some 250 years from 1670 to 1920.

Soon you change banks by crossing steeply humped Gallows Bridge **19**, a typical canal crossover bridge, made of iron in 1820. A high, battleship-grey bridge carries the Piccadilly Line, after which you pass under the M4 **Q** and into the London Borough of Ealing. The Capital Ring link to Boston Manor Station turns off here, but Walk 7 continues a further 200 yards to Osterley Lock **R**, crossing a concrete bridge onto an island formed by the separating river and canal. *Walk 8 continues along the towpath past Osterley Lock.*

***Capital Ring link with Boston Manor Station and buses****. Immediately after the M4 bridge **Q**, and before the concrete bridge, turn right along a rolled-gravel path which bends left to climb fairly steeply through woodland to a path junction. Continue ahead to a drive and walk along it between houses to the A3002 Boston Road **S**, opposite a Harvester pub-restaurant and close to bus stops. Turn right for 350 yards to Boston Manor Station **T**.*

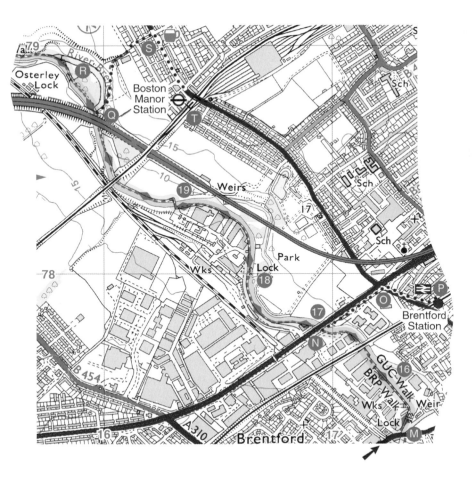

# 8 OSTERLEY LOCK TO GREENFORD

**Distance**: 4.8 miles (7.8 km). Excludes Capital Ring links 0.5 miles (0.8 km) from Boston Manor Station and 0.2 miles (0.3 km) to Greenford Station.

**Public transport.** The start of Walk 8 at Osterley Lock is 500 yards from bus stops on Boston Road and half a mile from Boston Manor Station. There is a Capital Ring link with Hanwell Station, and the route passes South Greenford Station. The finish at Greenford is 300 yards from the station and bus stops. All places on this walk are in Travelcard and Bus Zone 4.

**Surface and terrain.** The first and last miles are mostly on level tarmac, paving or bonded gravel, with some short, gentle ascents. The central section of 2 miles, from Hanwell Bridge to Greenford Bridge, is mostly on grass or earth paths, which may be muddy in places, or even under water after long periods of heavy rain. The link from Boston Manor Station is partly along a gently descending earth and gravel path.

**Refreshments**: Boston Manor, Hanwell Bridge, Brent Lodge Park, Greenford Bridge and Greenford Station.

**Toilets**: Boston Manor Station, Brent Lodge Park and Greenford Bridge.

*Capital Ring link from Boston Manor Station (0.5 miles / 0.8 km). From Boston Manor Station A turn left along Boston Road, crossing Wellmeadow Road, with bus stops nearby. In a further 250 yards, opposite the Harvester pub-restaurant, turn left along a tarmac footpath B. Shortly cross Southdown Avenue and continue ahead along a driveway. Go ahead through a gap in the fence, then bear left along a path between fences and past a sports pavilion. At a path junction, keep ahead to descend an earth then gravel path amid woodland. As you reach the M4 bridge C and the Grand Union Canal, turn right across a concrete bridge. Here you join the Capital Ring, briefly on Walk 7, to the official starting point of Walk 8.*

Walk 8 starts at Osterley Lock **D** in the London Borough of Ealing, where the Capital Ring still shares its route with the Grand Union Canal Walk and the Brent River Park Walk. As you continue along the canal towpath, the M4 mercifully swings away to the left. Though it can still be heard, the motorway passes out of sight, and there is a surprisingly rural feel to this area. To the right, the River Brent parts company with the canal again, flowing over a labyrinthine weir whose concertina design allows a greater flow of water in a confined space. A canalside pond soon afterwards is thick with reed mace.

The canal snakes between an industrial estate to the left and, to the right, Elthorne Waterside **1**, a former refuse tip that has been grassed over and is now a nature conservation area. Pass under Trumpers Way

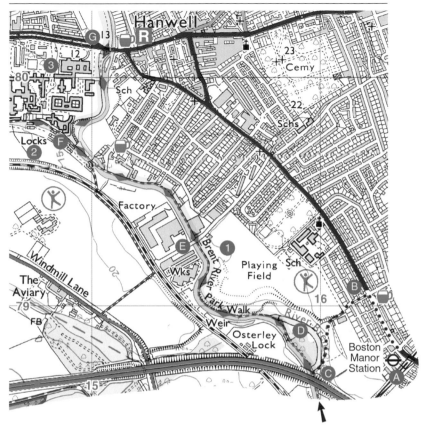

**E**, then a plaque beside the 'Braunston 91 miles' post records that this was the site of the Ealing Canal Celebration in 1993, when scores of narrow boats moored up here. A group of houses marks the start of Hanwell. The towpath crosses a bridge over the River Brent, which here makes its first rendezvous with the canal. Ahead now lies the Hanwell Flight **2** of six locks, created in 1794, which raise the canal 53 feet in 600 yards. Between the first and second lock **F**, you leave the Grand Union Canal, which continues ahead to Birmingham, but continue with the Brent River Park Walk. Soon after the first lock, turn right to follow a rolled-gravel path among trees beside the River Brent. This is known as Fitzherbert Walk, after Luke Fitzherbert, a leading light in the formation of the Brent River Park.

To your left now is the extensive Ealing Hospital **3**. In 400 yards, beside a small island formed by a side stream, you reach Hanwell Bridge **G** and A4020 Uxbridge Road. There has been a bridge at this point since the 14th century; the present one dates from 1762 and was

*At Hanwell, six locks raise the Grand Union Canal 53 feet in 600 yards.*

widened in 1906. You should be able to avoid crossing the road by passing under the old bridge, but if this is underwater you may prefer to cross the road at traffic lights to the right. You continue on grass along a field, with the river below to your right and the striking Wharncliffe Viaduct **4** ahead. The viaduct carries the Great Western Railway over the Brent valley. It was named after Lord Wharncliffe, who steered the GWR bill through the House of Lords, and whose coat of arms adorns the centre. As part of the GWR, the viaduct was designed by Isambard Kingdom Brunel and completed in 1838. At the end of the field, bear right to cross a footbridge over the river. Turn left under the viaduct and follow the path through a kissing gate **H** into Brent Lodge Park **5**, where the Capital Ring turns left down a slope.

*Capital Ring link with Hanwell Station (0.3 miles/0.4 km). After the kissing gate, go ahead up a tarmac path, then turn right at the junction. Follow this path between fences to the road and keep ahead to the railway bridge **I**. Do not go under it, but cross the road with care via the bollard at the central pier. On the far side, turn left along a road called Golden Manor, then in 80 yards turn right along Campbell Road. Follow this for 150 yards around a bend to Hanwell Station **J**. If starting here, from the station exit go ahead then left along Campbell Road. At the junction with Golden Manor, turn left to the railway bridge **I** and cross the road carefully to the right via the central bollard. Keep ahead to follow a tarmac footpath between fences. In 150 yards, at the end of a row of houses, turn left down a narrower path towards the viaduct, then turn right before the gate **H** down a slope.*

Brent Lodge Park used to be the grounds of a now-demolished mansion, home to the rectors of Hanwell. Follow the park fence on a tarmac path, uneven in places, with the river to your left. To your right, on the hilltop site of the original Hanwell village, rises the spire of St

Mary's Church **6**. Built in 1841, it was one of the earliest creations of eminent architect George Gilbert Scott. In 150 yards you pass through a double gate **K**, then turn left off the path to climb a short flight of shallow steps onto grass. The route officially follows the bends of the River Brent — no short cuts, please — as it swings round the west side of the park, though trees may hide it when in full leaf. On your right, behind a brick wall, is the Millennium Maze, planted in 2000 with yew bushes: when they are high enough, the maze could keep you occupied for a while. Further on, to your right beside a playground, are an animal centre **7** and clocktower, with toilets and a seasonal café, built in 1937 to commemorate the coronation of King George VI. Soon after a green pipe over the river and a dip in the ground, you bend right towards the church. Descend steps on your left to pass through a gap in the fence to a path junction **L**. *To visit the church, climb the earth path to the right for 100 yards.* Ahead lies Boles Meadow, a bird sanctuary where willow for basket-making is grown.

Cross the bridge over the river, then turn right on the main path across the meadow, with a sports field to your left. Keep to the gravel path as it touches the river again and then crosses Brent Valley Golf Course **8**. Ignore the path on the left and keep ahead, following a sheltered route among bushes — though you should still watch out for stray golf balls. After a stretch amid shrubbery, with low fences to each side, turn right by a Brent River Park post to cross a wooden footbridge **M** over the river.

Turn left and once more follow the east bank, briefly diverting around a reed-filled inlet. The riverside can get very wet and muddy here, so the route climbs steps up a bramble-covered bank onto a meadow, another grassed-over former refuse tip, prettily named Bitterns Field **9** – though you are unlikely to see such rare birds hereabouts. Follow the bank, parallel with the river, to the end of the meadow, then descend more steps back to the riverside. Turn right along the river bank, past a fenced playing field, to reach Greenford Bridge **N** on B455 Ruislip Road East. *There is no pedestrian crossing here, so if the road is busy you should cross at the lights, 150 yards to the right.*

You now part company with the Brent River Park Walk, which turns right with the river, while the Capital Ring continues northwards. Turn left over the Brent to a grassy strip, then sharp right along Costons Lane, using the left-hand pavement. Shortly after the road bears left, cross over and turn right along a track, which leads past a barrier **O** into Perivale Park **10**. Part of the riverside flood plain, its meadows are managed in traditional style to provide a wildlife haven. Cross Costons Brook, then bear left past Perivale Park Golf Course. The path veers left again to a park exit **P**. Do not go through; instead, turn right beside a bowling green. At the athletics track, bear half-left to a small car park, then keep ahead across a side road onto the A40 Western Avenue **Q**. To your right is South Greenford Station **R** on the little branch line from West Ealing to Greenford, a comparatively late addition to the railway network, opened in 1904 for the Great Western Railway.

Cross Western Avenue via the ramped footbridge. At the foot of the ramp on the far side, turn left along the side road, then shortly turn right along Cayton Road. At the end, by Northolt Rugby Football Club **S**, turn right along a paved footpath, which goes around Cayton Road Sports Ground **11**. Keep ahead at a path junction and continue to the far end. Turn right between posts into Bennetts Avenue **T** and follow it past Downing Drive, bearing left to reach A4127 Greenford Road **U**. Turn right under the viaduct and railway bridge, which carries the Central Line's West Ruislip branch and the Paddington to Birmingham railway line. Walk 8 ends at the junction with Rockware Avenue **V**, named after the great glassware manufacturers, now moved elsewhere, who dominated this area for many decades. To your right is the Westway Shopping Park **12**. *If continuing on to Walk 9, keep ahead across Rockware Avenue at the traffic lights.*

**Capital Ring link to Greenford Station** *(0.2 miles / 0.3 km). Turn left across Greenford Road at the traffic lights and go ahead along Rockware Avenue, passing bus stops. At the end, opposite the Railway pub, turn left along Oldfield Lane, passing under the bridge, to find the station entrance **W** on your right.*

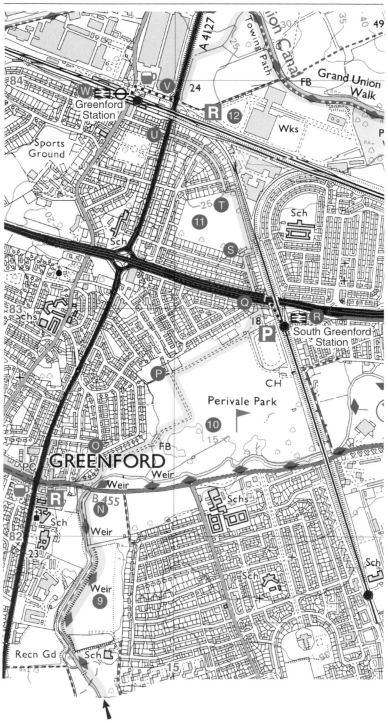

# 9 Greenford to South Kenton

**Distance**: 5.3 miles (8.5 km). Excludes Capital Ring link of 0.2 miles (0.3 km) from Greenford Station.

**Public transport**. The start of Walk 9 is 250 yards from Greenford Station and its bus stops. The route passes Sudbury Hill and Sudbury Hill Harrow Stations, and there are Capital Ring links with Harrow-on-the-Hill and Northwick Park Stations. It finishes at South Kenton Station, with a bus stop nearby. All places on this walk are in Travelcard and Bus Zone 4, but if you travel by train or tube to Harrow-on-the-Hill Station, this is in Zone 5.

**Surface and terrain**. This is one of the hilliest parts of the Capital Ring. A substantial amount is on uneven ground or grass, which may be muddy or wet after heavy rain, and there is one stile to climb over. There are two long and quite steep ascents and descents, over Horsenden Hill and through Harrow-on-the-Hill.

**Refreshments**: Greenford, Horsenden Hill, Sudbury Hill, Harrow-on-the-Hill and South Kenton.

**Toilets**: Horsenden Hill Visitor Centre.

***Capital Ring link from Greenford Station*** *(0.2 miles / 0.3 km). From the station exit **A** in Oldfield Lane, go over the zebra crossing ahead and turn left under the bridge. Turn right along Rockware Avenue, passing the station bus stops. Cross at the lights over Greenford Road towards Westway Shopping Park. You join the Capital Ring by turning left here.*

*A narrow boat on the Grand Union Canal near Paradise Fields Wetlands.*

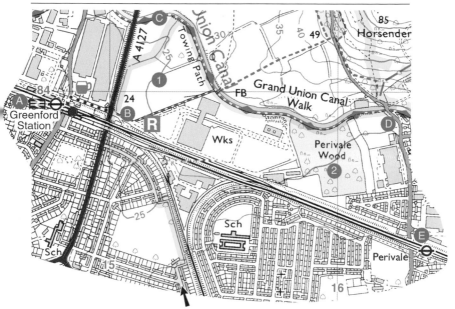

Walk 9 starts by crossing Rockware Avenue **B** at its junction with Greenford Road, in the London Borough of Ealing. Keep ahead past the Westway Shopping Park sign along a tarmac footpath/cycle track, with Greenford Road on your left and a car park on your right. The track dips into a subway and emerges in a nature reserve called Paradise Fields Wetlands **1**, where dogs must be kept on a lead. Converted from the former Greenford Golf Course, it contains several ponds and provides a good habitat for wildlife — lapwing have bred here recently. Passing a pond with a viewing platform, you see rising beyond it Horsenden Hill, which you will soon be climbing.

The route bears right on a bonded-gravel path across a meadow, with the West Ruislip branch of the Central Line on an embankment away to the right. The path soon rises to a footbridge **C**. Do not cross it; instead bear left through a gate to be reunited with the Grand Union Canal — this time the branch from Paddington Basin. Turn right under the bridge, and follow the towpath for half a mile as the canal swings back and forth, now with Horsenden Hill to your left. Further on, the trees of Perivale Wood Local Nature Reserve **2** lie to your right. A blank warehouse wall appears on the far bank, then you reach the old humped bridge **D** at Horsenden Lane North. Pass under it, then in 20 yards turn sharp right up four steps to the road. *Perivale Station **E** is 600 yards to the left here, but with no official Capital Ring link.* Turn right and cross over the new footbridge, added in 2002.

*An optional alternative route, adding some 300 yards, is provided here to Horsenden Hill Visitor Centre, which has a café, toilets and craft shops. For this, immediately past the bridge turn right through a wooden archway, then follow a rolled-gravel path beside the canal and past wooden sculptures. In 150 yards turn left through the car park up to the Horsenden Hill Visitor Centre **3**. The building to the left, formerly a farmhouse, now houses the rangers of Horsenden Hill. Continue uphill behind the big barn and through a gate. Keep ahead over a crossing path, then in 40 yards turn left beside a wire fence and small meadow, entering woodland. In 100 yards bear right with the main path to reach a larger meadow. At its end, keep ahead over a crossing path to the next junction **F**, where the main route comes up from the left. Skip the next paragraph.*

If you do not wish to visit the centre, the main route continues along the lane, crossing a drive. In 40 yards, turn right past a barrier, then immediately leave the tarmac path on an earth path bearing half-right into woodland. This climbs steeply on steps to emerge into the first of several meadows, which are ablaze with wild flowers in spring and summer. At a fork, keep ahead up to a T-junction by more trees **F** and very briefly turn left. The alternative route comes in from the right here.

Immediately after the junction, turn right up a narrow grass path climbing steeply between brambles to another meadow. This is one of the few places in the London area where dyers' greenweed grows: contradictorily, it was actually used to produce a yellow dye, then mixed with blue woad to produce green. Turn left and follow the path as it bears right, around bushes, then dives into a tunnel of bushes. This leads to a grassy terrace covering a reservoir. Keep ahead, then in 100 yards turn right, steeply uphill again, including steps, to the broad, grassy summit of Horsenden Hill **4**. This is one of the best natural viewpoints in Greater London. Another reservoir lies underneath, though this one is disused. Over to your right is a 'trig point' (concrete cairn), which marks the actual summit at altitude 260 feet. Trig is short for triangulation: these structures were once used by the Ordnance Survey for measurements, but have been replaced by satellite data.

Facing the trig-point cairn, turn left, then keep ahead on a broad, gently descending grass track. Shortly fork left, dropping more steeply into Horsenden Wood **5**. In 20 yards bear right between a fenced enclosure and a line of tree trunks down to a tarmac path. Turn right for 60 yards, then turn left along an earth path that runs parallel to garden fences to your right. This leads to a path junction at the end of Whitton Drive **G**. *Sudbury Town Station **H**, half a mile away, can be reached by turning right along this road, but there is no official Capital Ring link.* Turn left along a tarmac path, with trees to your left and grass to your right, and follow it for 400 yards back to Horsenden Lane North **I** at the Ballot Box pub.

Turn right along the pavement, opposite a rather sad row of shops, crossing Robin Hood Way and Drew Gardens. At the next junction, where Horsenden Lane North bears left, the Capital Ring goes ahead into Melville Avenue. All Hallows Church **6**, with its substantial brick tower, was built during World War II. Cross over at the refuge and continue in the same direction, now along the left-hand side. Cross Cambridge Avenue to reach A4090 Whitton Avenue East **K**. Turn left to cross at the traffic lights **L**, then turn right for 20 yards and left up Ridding Lane. At the end, by Allen Court, bear left along a broad tarmac footpath. You rejoin A4127 Greenford Road **M**, turning right over a railway line into the London Borough of Harrow.

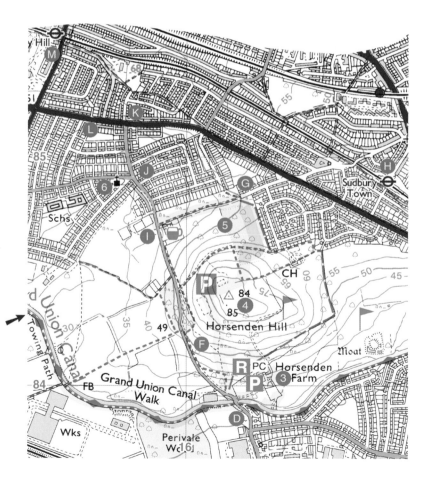

Cross at the lights by Sudbury Hill Station **N**, then turn right past a parade of shops, and after 200 yards you reach Sudbury Hill Harrow Station. In 30 yards, opposite the Rising Sun pub, turn left along South Vale **O**, keeping to the left-hand side for 300 yards. Up to your right, beyond a sports ground, the eye-catching white mansion **7** was built around 1820 as Sudbury Hill House. From 1929 to 1977 it was the sanatorium of Harrow School. The building was gutted by fire in 1980; it has since been absorbed into a residential development, incorporating part of the original façade. The tall green pipe halfway along South Vale carries fumes from an underground sewer well away from your nostrils. Where the road turns left as Wood End Road **P**, cross over with great care, as traffic approaches quite fast. You should position yourself at the bend, where you can see and be seen by traffic approaching both ways.

Turn right up a stony historic track called Green Lane, which climbs steeply, with houses to your left and a field to your right. During the 19th century, this was part of the road linking Harrow with Greenford. At the top, cross South Hill Avenue **Q** and keep ahead up the left-hand pavement of A4005 Sudbury Hill, with substantial houses on either side reflecting the long-standing prosperity of this area. At the top, where Sudbury Hill becomes London Road, and just before the junction with Mount Park Avenue **R**, cross carefully at the refuge and continue in the same direction along the right-hand pavement. Where the main road bends left **S**, keep ahead, still in London Road, to the little square **T** (actually more of a triangle) at the centre of the old village of Harrow-on-the-Hill. At an altitude of 350 feet (105 metres), you are now at one of the highest points of the Capital Ring. And at 10 miles (16 km) from Charing Cross, this is as far from the centre as the Capital Ring gets. The hill, though compact, is isolated and can be seen for miles. It is thought to have been a place of pagan worship in prehistoric times, and the Saxon origin of the name Harrow means 'sacred grove'. Here, in 1094, the Normans built one of their earliest English churches, St Mary's **10**, which still stands, though much altered. Its spire, one of the highest points in North London, identifies the hill from afar.

The historic King's Head Hotel **8** beside the square was closed awaiting redevelopment at the time of writing. It claims to date from 1535 and to be one of the places where Henry VIII courted Anne Boleyn, but the earliest documentary reference is in 1706. Continue past the square along the High Street. You are now among the scattered, mainly red-brick buildings of Harrow School **9**. Founded in 1572, it started with just one pupil, but its reputation grew steadily,

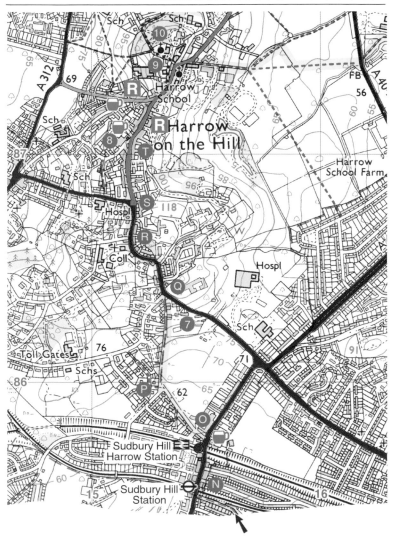

and from the early 19th century the school was educating future statesmen such as Winston Churchill and Pandit Nehru, and great writers such as Byron, Sheridan and Trollope. Ahead lies the flint-dressed school chapel, consecrated in 1857, with the chapel-like Vaughan Library of 1863 set back just before it. Up to your left in Church Hill, the red-brick building with a clocktower is the original school, dating from 1615. Beyond that rises the spire of St Mary's **10**, whose set of ten bells may accompany you through Harrow at times of services and celebration.

*Capital Ring link with Harrow-on-the-Hill Station (0.6 miles / 0.9 km). Just before the Harrow School bus stop **U**, cross over at a width restrictor, turn right then immediately bear left up Church Hill to the lych gate of St Mary's. Go through it and turn left along a tarmac path, past the church door. At a path junction, turn right to descend steeply past graves to the end of a road called Roxborough Park **V**. Shortly turn right along a fenced tarmac footpath, and on reaching The Grove Open Space bear half-left down to A404 Lowlands Road **W**. Turn left to the traffic lights, cross and turn right, then left along Station Road to climb 26 steps into Harrow-on-the-Hill Station **X**.*

*If starting here, bear in mind that the link to the Capital Ring involves a long and sometimes very steep climb. From the ticket barriers, turn left to the car-park exit and go ahead to A404 Lowlands Road. Turn right to cross at the lights, then turn left along the far side, beside The Grove Open Space. In 150 yards jink sharp right up a narrow tarmac path **W**, then turn sharp left, so that you are climbing towards the church spire. At the top, bear right along a fenced tarmac path. Turn left at the road, Roxborough Park **V**, and keep ahead up a wide but very steep tarmac path, with graves to your right. At the top, turn left into the churchyard, pass the church door and turn right through the lych gate. Go down Church Hill, then, opposite the Old School Building, turn left and left again down the white ceremonial steps to the High Street. Turn left and go over the zebra crossing to join the Capital Ring opposite the Speech Room **Y**.*

The Capital Ring continues along the High Street, opposite the school's Speech Room **Y** of 1877, described by Pevsner as being of partly Sicilian Gothic style. Bear right down Peterborough Road, then shortly turn right into the aptly named Football Lane **Z** (signed 'Public Footpath to Watford Road'), beside the Museum of Harrow Life. This leads steeply down to Harrow School's playing fields. On the way you pass its Music School **11** of 1890, which bears the white-lion coat of arms of John Lyon, the local farmer who founded Harrow School. In the private car park at the bottom a signpost points ahead to Watford Road, but as this direct path crosses sports pitches which may be in use, and may not be easy to follow, Harrow School has agreed a diversion. In the car park **AA**, turn left along a gravel track for 200 yards, then turn right to follow a line of trees **AB** along a gentle grass bank. At an area of wild grass **AC**, turn left along its edge — but don't miss the classic view back to the school on the hill. Coming to the corner of a playing field, follow a well-hidden path ahead to cross a stile — the only one on the whole Capital Ring — onto A404 Watford Road **AD**. The route continues along a footpath opposite, called the Ducker Path, but as this road is very busy you should only cross at this point if traffic is light. Otherwise, turn left for 200 yards to cross at the lights by the entrance to Northwick Park Hospital, returning along the far side.

Now in the London Borough of Brent, follow the Ducker Path into a wood. It takes its name from the former outdoor swimming pool of Harrow School, where Sir Winston Churchill swam as a boy. It leads into Northwick Park **12**, soon coming to the extensive buildings of Northwick Park and St Mark's Hospitals **13**. Continue through a long meadow, still beside the hospitals, at the end of which you cross a stream **AE**. Turn right along the tarmac Proyer's Path.

***Capital Ring link with Northwick Park Station*** *(0.4 miles / 0.6 km). After crossing the stream, turn left along Proyer's Path for 600 yards, passing the hospital and a University of Middlesex building. The park entrance to Northwick Park Station* ***AF*** *lies a little to the right. If starting here, from the ticket barriers turn left, directly into the park. Take the first path to the left, keeping tall chimneys to your right, and follow it for 600 yards, passing the end of the hospital fence to a footbridge* ***AE***, *where you join the Capital Ring.*

Keep ahead through a car park, with a pavilion over to your left, and walk on grass to the left of its approach road. Just before the park exit **AG**, turn left, still on grass, to follow the park edge towards the railway, which is the West Coast Main Line **14** from Euston to the North West and Scotland, with the Bakerloo Line alongside. This section into Hertfordshire was one of the earliest railway lines in Britain, opened in 1837. It was extended to Birmingham in 1838 and Glasgow in 1848, becoming the famous LMS (London Midland and Scottish Railway) in 1923. Shortly before the railway, turn right into Nathans Road **AH**, then in 40 yards turn left into a cul-de-sac (The Link), which leads to the subway of South Kenton Station **AI**, the end of Walk 9. The ticket office and platforms are up 30 steps to the right. *Walk 10 continues through the subway.*

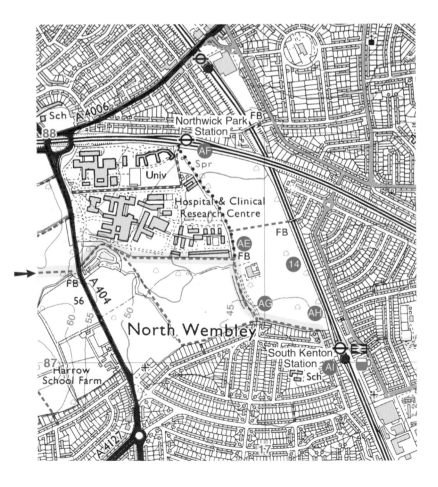

*One of the highest points in North London, the spire of St Mary's in Harrow-on-the-Hill can be seen from miles around.*

# 10 SOUTH KENTON TO HENDON PARK

**Distance**: 5.9 miles (9.6 km). Excludes Capital Ring link of 0.4 miles (0.7 km) to Hendon Central Station.

**Public transport**. The start of Walk 9 is at South Kenton Station, with bus stops nearby. The route passes Preston Road Station, and there are links with Wembley Park and Hendon Stations. The finish in Hendon Park is just under half a mile from Hendon Central Station and buses. The section from South Kenton to Church Lane, Kingsbury, is Zone 4. West Hendon Broadway and Brent Cross are Zone 3. Hendon and Hendon Central Stations are in both Zones 3 and 4.

**Surface and terrain**. Mostly fairly level on tarmac, paving or bonded gravel, but the 2-mile central section through Fryent Country Park is on uneven or grassy paths, steep in places, which may be wet or muddy.

**Refreshments**: South Kenton, Preston Road, near Brent Reservoir, West Hendon Broadway and Hendon Central.

**Toilets**: Near Brent Reservoir.

*The pond at the summit of Barn Hill was created by the landscape designer Humphry Repton. In early summer an army of tiny frogs emerges.*

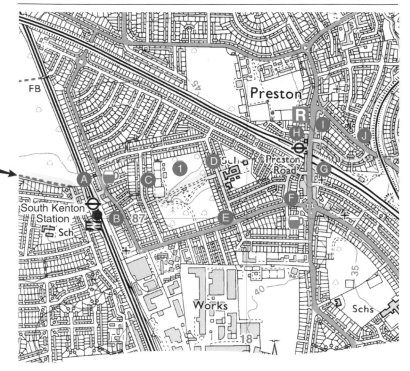

Walk 10 starts in the subway **A** under South Kenton Station, in the London Borough of Brent. From the platform, turn right at the foot of the steps out of the subway, then jink right and left past the Windermere pub. Cross Windermere Avenue and turn right, then in 70 yards turn left into Allonby Gardens **B**. At the end, go half-right along an alleyway leading to Montpelier Rise **C**. Cross over and turn right, then in 50 yards turn left past a barrier into Preston Park **1**.

Go straight ahead through the park to College Road **D**, then cross over and turn right, past Preston Park Primary School. In 125 yards, turn left along Glendale Gardens **E**. At the end, turn left into Longfield Avenue **F**, cross Grasmere Avenue at the bottom, then turn right up to the busy Preston Road **G**. Turn left past Preston Road Station **H** and bus stops. Cross at the lights, turn left then right into Uxendon Crescent **I**; Uxendon is the name of the farm and hamlet that once occupied this area. Poking up above the houses ahead is the little stone-domed tower of the Parish Church of the Ascension **2**. At the end, turn right along The Avenue **J** and cross over at the refuge. Continue under the railway bridge, which carries the Jubilee Line to Stanmore.

With the parish church ahead again, bear left up West Hill **K** at the grass patch, crossing Wealdstone Brook, which flows into the River Brent. In 60 yards turn left along Uxendon Hill and follow it round for 350 yards to turn left along a grassy path between numbers 79 and 81 **L**. This leads into Fryent Country Park **3**, where for the next couple of miles you will be walking on grass or earth paths, which may be wet and muddy, and climbing quite steeply in places. However, the surroundings and views are well worth the effort. Fryent Country Park is a large nature reserve encompassing two high points, Barn Hill and Gotfords Hill, and a huge swathe of countryside where natural features are preserved as they have been for centuries. The park is divided into two by Fryent Way, with woodland dominating the western part and open grassland the east.

Keep ahead among trees and bushes, with the Jubilee Line to your left. On reaching a large meadow, stay beside the railway for 100 yards to a footbridge **M**, then turn right uphill to the left-hand corner of the meadow. Keep ahead into the wood and follow the main broad earth path all the way to the pond at the top of Barn Hill **4**. Follow the path along the right-hand side of the pond and go on a few yards to a white trig point **N**, which marks the summit. At an altitude of 282 feet (85 metres), Barn Hill has long been a favoured viewpoint. You should have a fine view across West London, with the twin towers of Wembley Stadium prominent — if they are still standing following redevelopment — and, on a clear day, the North Downs in the distance.

*Capital Ring link with Wembley Park Station (0.7 miles / 1.2 km). At the trig point **N**, turn left down a broad grassy track to a small car park and information board. Keep ahead along the road, also called Barn Hill, following the left-hand pavement all the way down to A4088 Forty Lane **O**. Cross at the lights, turning right and left to continue in the same direction along the right-hand side of Bridge Road for 300 yards to Wembley Park Station **P**. If starting from here, at the station exit turn left for 300 yards along Bridge Road to Forty Lane **O**. Turn right then left across the lights and continue in the same direction up the right-hand side of Barn Hill all the way to the top. Go past the information board, then bear half-left up a broad grassy track to the white trig point **N**.*

From the trig point, return to the pond and follow the path on its right-hand side. You do not quite complete the circuit: at the far end, 30 yards away from the path you came up by, keep ahead down a steep path, taking care over some exposed roots. Go all the way down, ignoring two crossing paths. You come to a field at the bottom **Q**, where there is a good view northwards over Kingsbury. Turn right along a path through the trees, with the field to your left. In 250 yards you reach an intersection between fields, where a signpost reveals that the crossing track is called Eldestrete **R**. It is thought that this ancient road dates from pre-Roman times and was used by pilgrims to St Alban's shrine. *If you need to get to Kingsbury Station **S** (0.8 miles / 1.3 km off route), you can follow Eldestrete to the left, continuing along Fryent Way, though this is not an official Capital Ring link.*

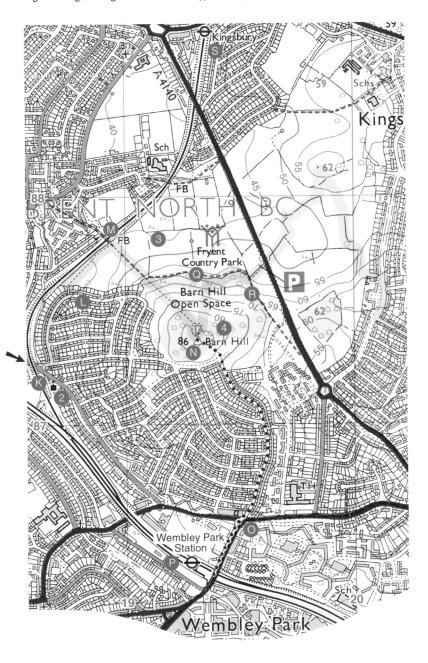

The route continues half-left across grass, passing a park information board, into a small car park. At the exit, pass under the height restrictor to A4140 Fryent Way **T**. There is no controlled crossing and the road is very busy, so take great care as you cross it to a gap in the bank opposite. Bear half-left beside a hedgerow, then go to the left of a small pond into the next field. Follow the hedgerow along the left-hand side of this large field as it bends right. At the far left-hand corner, turn left through a gap in the hedge and keep ahead across the next small field, now with the hedgerow on your right. Carry on through another gap, then climb towards the left-hand side of two lonely ash trees on the skyline, beside a marker post. Forty yards short of the tree, you turn right on a clear path **U**, but you can keep on to the summit if you wish and then return to this point to continue on the Capital Ring. From the rounded summit of Gotfords Hill, you have a magnificent 360-degree panorama over much of North and North-west London. To the west, you should be able to see Harrow-on-the-Hill, from Walk 9, with the spire of St Mary's Church.

Having turned right, follow the path to the field corner, a little to the right of two tall, black Italian poplar trees. Go through a gap and keep ahead, with a paddock fence just to your left and Fryent Way running parallel away to the right. At the end of the field, you pass through a gap to find yourself facing a hedge end **V**. Turn right then immediately left into the next field, so that the hedgerow is now to your left, and follow the left-hand side of this field, still with Fryent Way parallel to your right. At the end, cross a ditch into the next field, turn left and follow the hedgerow. In 50 yards, with houses ahead, turn right, still in the same field with the hedgerow to your left. At the top, before a small copse, turn left in front of a signpost and head for a brick wall. Go to the left of it along a grass track between fences, and pass a barrier to arrive on Salmon Street **W**, in a residential part of Kingsbury.

It is hoped that the route will eventually follow a greener and more direct route to Brent Reservoir, but for the present it follows roads, as described here. Cross Salmon Street, then turn right along the pavement. Cross Mallard Way, then in 150 yards, as the road swings right, turn left along Lavender Avenue **X**. Soon after the road veers left, turn right down Holden Avenue **Y**. At the end, cross Dunster Drive **Z** and turn left into B454 Church Lane **AA**. Turn right for 50 yards, then cross over at the refuge by Wells Drive, continuing along the opposite side of Church Lane. Just before the bend, you pass the new St Andrew's Church **5** on your left, with its tall stone spire. The 'new' St Andrew's Church was built in 1847 in Wells Street, Marylebone, and was well known in its day for musical perfor-

mances. After lying redundant for some years, in 1931 it was moved here, stone by stone, to become the parish church of Kingsbury, adjacent to and replacing the old St Andrew's. The interior is quite striking, giving the impression of a small cathedral.

Bear left into Old Church Lane **AB**, passing some gravestones in the old churchyard. At the next bend **AC**, turn left, still in Old Church Lane, cross over and turn left along the pavement behind a grass bank, with old St Andrew's **6** to your left — now closed and rather forlorn among shrubs and beautiful yew trees at the centre of the graveyard. This is rich in wildlife and has been designated a 'Site of Borough Importance for Nature Conservation'.

Soon after a right-hand bend, you cross Birchen Close and pass a barrier. Turn left along Birchen Grove **AD**, then turn right at a bend **AE**. *There are toilets 300 yards ahead through the gate at the Greenhouse Garden Centre **7**, which also has a café.* At the end of the road **AF**, pass a car park to your right. Go half-right along a tarmac track past a barrier

*This pond occupies a World War II bomb crater beside Brent Reservoir. Often the reservoir is criss-crossed by a flotilla of sailing dinghies.*

and a black interpretative kiosk, then Brent Reservoir **8** shimmers into view. It is known locally as the Welsh Harp, after a pub that used to stand nearby. Built in 1883 to supply water to the Regent's Canal, it is one of the largest sheets of water in Greater London, at nearly a mile in length and a quarter of a mile across at its widest point. The reservoir and its surroundings are a naturalists' paradise: fauna recorded over the years include nearly 250 species of bird and 200 species of moth. For a while, this was one of London's leading visitor attractions, with its own railway station nearby, though this closed in 1903, and the rowing events of the 1948 Olympic Games were held here.

The level track runs along the gently sloping parkland on the north bank of the reservoir, while the land beyond the south bank has been colonised by large commercial complexes. In 400 yards, where tarmac gives way to bonded gravel, you enter the London Borough of Barnet. A pond to your right lies in a World War II bomb crater. Approaching the end, a breeze-block wall to your left protects you from a rifle range — red flags warn that shooting is in progress. Pass the wooden cabins and slipway of the North Circular Sailing Club, then at a fork keep right past a car park. A viewing platform appears on your right, overlooking the northward spur of the reservoir **9**, formed from the Silk Stream. Keep on to Cool Oak Lane **AG** and cross over carefully. The detached part of the reservoir beyond has the appearance of a seaside creek, with dinghies moored at the Welsh Harp Youth Sailing Base opposite.

Turn right across the narrow bridge, but as this has no pavement you must await your turn: press the pedestrians' button and wait for the green walking man to light up. Continue along the left-hand side of Cool Oak Lane for 300 yards to reach A5 West Hendon Broadway **AH**. Cross at the lights and turn left for 30 yards to reach the junction with Park Road **AI**, where the Capital Ring turns right. The dead-straight A5 is a continuation of Watling Street, the old Roman road that you encountered on Walk 1, which headed from Londinium through Verulamium (St Albans) to the fortress of Viroconium (Wroxeter) on the Welsh border.

*Capital Ring link to Hendon Station* (0.3 miles / 0.5 km). At Park Road **AI**, keep ahead along West Hendon Broadway for 200 yards. At the next traffic lights, turn right up Station Road **AJ** and follow it around to the zebra crossing by Hendon Station **AK**. If starting here, from the station exit turn right up to Station Road and go over the zebra crossing. Turn right down to the traffic lights, then turn left along West Hendon Broadway **AJ** for 200 yards to Park Road **AI**, where you cross over and turn left.

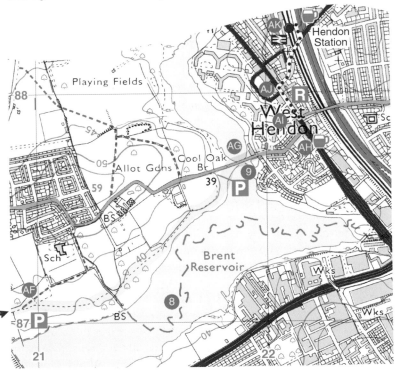

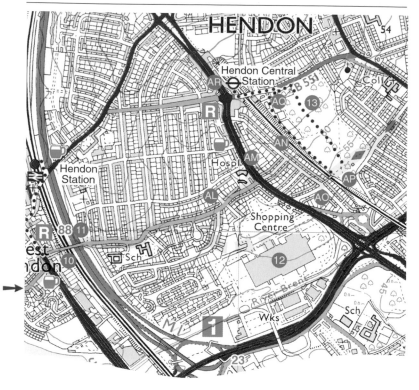

The Capital Ring follows Park Road across the main railway line **10** from St Pancras to the East Midlands and Yorkshire, opened in 1868 for the Midland Railway, which now also carries Thameslink trains. Welsh Harp Station, now demolished, lay to the right of the bridge. Then comes the M1 **11**, Britain's first motorway, opened in 1959, although this section is a southward extension opened in 1974. During World War II, this area reverberated with the sound of warplanes using Hendon Aerodrome, a mile to the north. This was one of Britain's first aviation centres, famed for its air displays between the wars. Though the airfield is now closed, parts of its grounds are occupied by the RAF Museum and the Hendon Police Training Centre.

Park Road rises and falls, snaking past Parkfield Junior Mixed Infants School and some drastically pollarded trees. After crossing the brow of the hill, on your right you may glimpse the high concrete walls and car-park lights of the huge Brent Cross Shopping Centre **12**, Britain's first major shopping mall, opened in 1976, which claims to house over 100 top retailers under one roof. *If this is irresistible, you can reach it by turning right at Sturgess Avenue **AL**, then in 150 yards turn left along a footpath through a small public garden. You can finish the walk here, if you wish, as the centre has its own bus station (0.4 miles / 0.7 km off route).* Otherwise, continue along Park Road as it bears left uphill to A41 Hendon Way **AM**, and cross it in a ramped subway to the left.

Hendon has a connection with David Garrick, the great 18th-century actor. At a time when being 'lord of the manor' was still a real status symbol, he bought the ancient manor of Hendon at auction. The land had previously belonged to the Herbert family, later the Earls of Pembroke and Marquises of Powys.

On the far side of the subway, turn right up the ramp, then turn left along Beaufort Gardens. At the end, cross and turn right along Cheyne Walk **AN**. In 200 yards, at the junction with Renters Avenue **AO**, turn left along a tarmac path and climb 23 steps up and down to cross a footbridge over the Northern Line's Edgware branch. The bridge leads into Hendon Park **13**, where Walk 10 finishes 40 yards ahead at a path junction **AP**. *Walk 11 continues ahead along the path with lampposts.*

***Capital Ring link to Hendon Central Station*** *(0.5 miles / 0.8 km). At the path junction **AP**, turn left on grass, parallel with an avenue of trees. At the crossing path, continue ahead, now between the trees. At the top, turn left along a tarmac path for 80 yards to the park exit. Leave the park and turn left along Queen's Road **AQ** to the traffic lights at Hendon Way, where you cross right to Hendon Central Station **AR**. In wet weather, you can avoid the grass by turning left at the foot of the steps from the footbridge along a tarmac path beside the railway. Follow the path all the way to the top, past tennis courts, then turn right towards the Memorial Garden and leave the park via Queen's Road **AQ** to continue as above.*

# 11 HENDON PARK TO HIGHGATE

**Distance**: 5.1 miles (8.2 km). Excludes Capital Ring links of 0.4 miles (0.7 km) from Hendon Central Station and 0.1 miles (0.1 km) to Highgate Station.

**Public transport**. The start of Walk 11 is in Hendon Park, just under half a mile from Hendon Central Station and buses. The route passes East Finchley Station. The finish is in Priory Gardens, 120 yards from Highgate Station. All places on this walk are in Travelcard and Bus Zone 3, except Hendon Central, which is in both Zones 3 and 4.

**Surface and terrain**. Most of the route is on paving, tarmac or bonded gravel, and generally fairly level. The central section of half a mile includes some uneven paths with short but fairly steep ascents and descents, and the last half-mile in Queen's Wood is on steep earth paths, which can be avoided by following nearby roads.

**Refreshments**: Hendon Central, Temple Fortune, Hampstead Garden Suburb, East Finchley, Cherry Tree Wood, Highgate Wood, Queen's Wood and Highgate.

**Toilets**: Lyttelton Playing Fields, Cherry Tree Wood and Highgate Wood.

*Capital Ring link from Hendon Central Station. From the station exit **A**, turn left and cross at the traffic lights. Turn left up Queen's Road, over the railway and past some of the station bus stops. In 150 yards, turn right into Hendon Park **B**. Immediately turn left along a tarmac path, parallel to the road, then in 80 yards, past the end of a hedge, turn right to walk on grass down an avenue of trees. At a crossing path keep ahead, still on grass, with the avenue of trees on your right, to a path junction **C** with Capital Ring signs. Here you join the Capital Ring by turning left along the broader path with lampposts. Walk 10 of the Capital Ring comes in from the right, across the footbridge. In wet weather, you can avoid the grass as follows: on entering Hendon Park, turn right to go around the tennis courts, then turn left on a tarmac path along the edge of the park to the footbridge mentioned above, where you turn left.*

Walk 11 of the Capital Ring starts in Hendon Park **1**, in the London Borough of Barnet. Leave the park and keep ahead along Shirehall Lane **D**. Pass Park View Gardens and Elms Avenue, then cross to the opposite pavement and take the next right turn into Shirehall Close **E**. At the end, turn left along Shirehall Park **F** and bear left with the road. In 40 yards turn right along a short link road, using the left-hand pavement, to reach A502 Brent Street **G**.

Cross Brent Street at the refuge and turn right. As you cross the River Brent, look left to see two pepperpot gazebos on either side of a weir. They survive from a time when the gardens on either side belonged to the Brent Bridge Hotel, demolished in 1974. Ahead lies

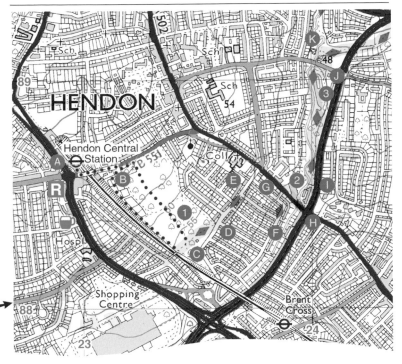

the A406 North Circular Road **H**, built during the 1920s, which has the dubious distinction of being the noisiest road in Britain and will make its presence felt for the next mile. Turn left beside it for 150 yards, then after Brook Lodge turn left through a gate **I** into Brent Park **2**. This is the first of several open spaces along this stretch of the Capital Ring, resulting from a policy of leaving such areas undeveloped in case of flooding. Ignoring the footbridge to your left, keep ahead for a few yards, then take the right fork. Soon you are walking among trees on a winding and gently undulating tarmac path, beside or close to the River Brent, with the North Circular Road to your right.

At the next path junction, turn sharp left around the end of a pond. You continue between the river and several ponds, collectively known as The Decoy **3**, where ducks were lured for capture — the surrounding woodland used to be called Decoy Wood. After the last pond, the path swings right, then you turn left to leave the park through a gate into Bridge Lane **J**. Cross over and turn left for 50 yards, then turn right beside the river along a tarmac path called Brookside Walk. You shortly reach the point **K** where Dollis Brook (from ahead) and Mutton Brook (from the right) merge to form the River Brent. Dollis Brook rises at Moat

*The ponds of The Decoy in Brent Park were once used to capture ducks for the dining table.*

Mount, near Scratchwood Services on the M1; Mutton Brook rises near Highgate. In 1996, the remains of a cayman — a type of alligator — were found near here in Dollis Brook; the poor beast had probably been dumped by a collector and left to cope in an unfavourable habitat.

For the next mile you join the Dollis Valley Greenwalk, which follows Dollis Brook from Moat Mount and Barnet, and then turns along Mutton Brook. Turn right along the narrow tarmac path beside Mutton Brook, keeping ahead through the short tunnel under the North Circular Road. The path gets even narrower, and in places the surface is uneven and may be muddy. It rises and falls beside a long, grassy open space, with the North Circular Road now to your left. Eventually, you rise quite steeply to reach A598 Finchley Road at Henly's Corner.

Cross Finchley Road carefully at the traffic lights **L**. On the far side, look left, beyond the North Circular, for a distant view beyond a bus stop of a sculpture that has given this junction its unofficial local name: 'The Naked Lady' **4**. Its proper name is *La Délivrance*, by Emile Guillaume, and it commemorates the alliance of British and French troops at the Battle of the Marne in 1914. Turn right, then in 20 yards turn left down a steep tarmac path to continue in the same direction. Cross the footbridge over Mutton Brook and climb to the right of it, not quite reaching a road **M**. Bear left behind the houses, still close to the brook. At a path junction keep ahead, with Mutton Brook emerging from a culvert nearby, then turn right into Addison Way **N**. Turn left for 80 yards, then cross the road at a width restrictor. In 50 yards the Dollis Valley Greenwalk splits off to the right towards its eventual target, Hampstead Heath.

The Capital Ring continues ahead, now beside the A1 Falloden Way. After crossing Mutton Brook **O**, turn right along a tarmac path into Northway Gardens **5**, and follow it round to the left, with the brook to your right. At a path intersection, keep ahead towards a black shelter, left of the brook, with tennis courts on the far bank. At the shelter, bear right then left, staying on the brook's left bank. After more tennis courts, fork left to reach a road, Northway **P**, in Hampstead Garden Suburb. This settlement was the brainchild of Henrietta Barnett, a leading philanthropist and social reformer. In 1906, she set up a trust to acquire land in the area, partly to extend Hampstead Heath, but mostly to develop an integrated community, where people from all backgrounds could live in pleasant surroundings. This brave social experiment only lasted for a decade or two before commercial pressures took over; the area has since become one of the most affluent parts of London.

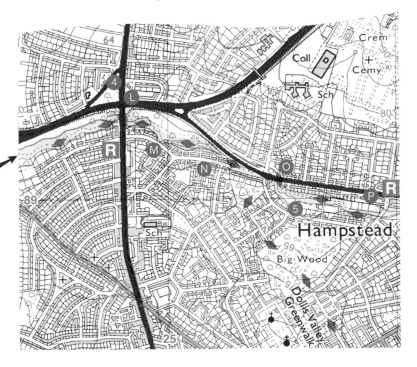

Cross Northway and keep ahead into the next part of Northway Gardens, with Mutton Brook still to your right. Cross Kingsley Way **Q** and turn right over the brook, then turn left past a barrier into Lyttelton Playing Fields **6**. You have now entered the territory of what used to be the Bishop of London's extensive hunting park, which was created in the 13th century and extended well to the east from here. At a fork, bear right, away from the brook, with the Barnet Children's Millennium Wood ahead, planted in 2000. The track bends left past a playground. At a pavilion (*with toilets*), the path swings left then right past tennis courts. After a bowling green, the path swings right then left to leave the park via a road called Norrice Lea **R**. Turn left, passing Hampstead Garden Suburb Synagogue, to reach A1 Lyttelton Road **S**.

*Queen's Wood near Highgate, once known as Churchyard Bottom Wood, was renamed in the late 19th century after Queen Victoria.*

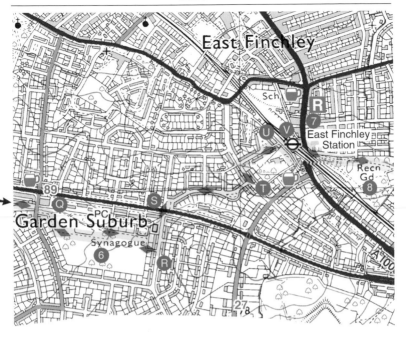

Cross at the lights, then turn right and immediately left into Vivian Way. Follow it round to the right, then in 250 yards you reach a little green, where the road swings left to reach Deansway **T**. Cross over and turn left, then in 80 yards turn right up Edmund's Walk. At the top, by another little green, keep ahead along a narrow path to a T-junction. Turn right along a broader path called The Causeway **U** to arrive at the back entrance of East Finchley Station **V**. You should be able to go through the station subway to the A1000 Great North Road. *If the subway is closed, continue along The Causeway to the Great North Road and turn left under the bridge to reach the traffic lights.* Look up above the station entrance to see *The Archer*, a bold statue firing an arrow along the railway line towards Highgate. Uphill, on the opposite side of the road, you can just see the sign of the venerable Phoenix Cinema **7**, opened in 1910 as the East Finchley Picturedrome. Cross over at the traffic lights. The Great North Road leads from London through Finchley to the north of England and eventually to Edinburgh, a distance of some 400 miles. From at least the 14th century, this was the main route to the north, replacing the Roman Ermine Street further east.

On the far side of the road, turn right. In 20 yards turn left between concrete bollards before the bridge, then bear right through a gate into a park called Cherry Tree Wood **8**. Unsurprisingly renamed from the original Dirthouse Wood, it is a remnant of the ancient Forest of Middlesex and of the Bishop of London's hunting park. Keep ahead along a tarmac path past a playground. Leave the park, passing toilets and a seasonal refreshment kiosk, and proceed ahead along Fordington Road **W**. At the junction with Woodside Avenue **X**, cross via a refuge and go up Lanchester Road opposite. In 50 yards turn left up a steep tarmac path between fences. At the top you cross the disused and overgrown track of the former branch line from Finsbury Park to Alexandra Palace, which later forms part of Walk 12 of the Capital Ring. Pass through Bridge Gate **Y** into Highgate Wood **9**, where the paths and tracks are formed from crushed stone. Highgate Wood, previously known as Gravel Pit Wood, is another remnant of the Forest of Middlesex. It is one of the many parcels of open space that were acquired by the Corporation of London during the 19th century so that they could be maintained in perpetuity for Londoners' recreation, at a time when any open space within reach of the City was under pressure for housing development.

Keep ahead on the path to an intersection **Z**. On the left is a functioning granite drinking fountain, erected in 1888, with separate troughs for horses and dogs. It bears a quotation from 'Inscription for a fountain on a heath', penned in 1802 by Samuel Taylor Coleridge. Turn right at the fountain along a dirt track to the next junction **AA**. *Just a few yards ahead are the park café and toilets.* The Capital Ring goes left, then keeps ahead at a junction to go past a lodge. Bear right, parallel to a road, then keep ahead at a crossing track and drop down leftwards to leave the woods through New Gate beside traffic lights. Cross B550 Muswell Hill Road **AB** and enter Queen's Wood **10**. The next section through Queen's Wood is very steep, on uneven paths and tracks; if you are prepared for this, skip the next paragraph.

*The steep paths of Queen's Wood can be avoided as follows. After crossing Muswell Hill Road **AB**, turn right along it for 400 yards to the traffic lights at Archway Road **AG**, where there are buses. For Highgate Station **AF** turn left for 150 yards to a London Underground sign, but you then have to descend a total of 101 steps in several flights to reach the station ticket office, or continue to the next road and turn sharp left through the car park. If continuing to Walk 12, keep on down Archway Road to rejoin the Capital Ring at the junction with Shepherd's Hill.*

Queen's Wood is a complete contrast to Highgate Wood: less visited, much hillier and an altogether wilder atmosphere, the result of careful planning by the London Borough of Haringey to maintain the natural balance. This used to be known as Churchyard Bottom Wood until the late 19th century, when it was acquired by Hornsey Council and renamed after Queen Victoria. Follow signs to Shepherd's Hill

and Crouch End. Go down the path to the Woodkeeper's Lodge **11**.
Built in 1898, the lodge has been taken on by CUE (Conservation and
Urban Ecology) in order to make it a showpiece of environmentally
friendly urban living. Food from the lodge's organic garden is served
in its café, open Fridays to Mondays. Bear right downhill, then at the
bottom, by a fence corner, go ahead to a signpost and bear right past
a heavily burled tree. You soon climb steeply uphill, bearing left and
levelling out at the top, only to rise again as the path bears right.

At the next path junction, keep ahead to Queen's Wood Road **AC**
and cross over to the next part of the wood. The path rises at first, then
drops downhill. Keep ahead at a crossing path and bear left to the foot
of the hill, by a low brick wall. Turn right up a steep tarmac path to the
road, Priory Gardens **AD**, and turn right. Walk 11 finishes in 250 yards,
opposite a narrow footpath between house numbers 63 and 65 **AE**. *To
continue on Walk 12, turn left up this path. For Highgate Station **AF**, continue ahead along Priory Gardens for 120 yards. For buses in Archway
Road, go through the station ticket office and up the escalator.*

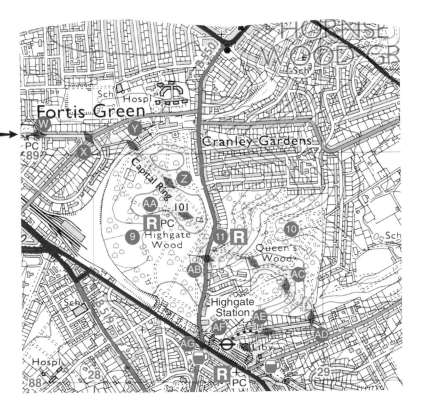

# 12 HIGHGATE TO STOKE NEWINGTON

**Distance**: 4.4 miles (7.1 km). Excludes Capital Ring links of 0.1 miles (0.1 km) at each end.

**Public transport**. The start of Walk 12 is 120 yards from Highgate Station. The route passes Manor House Station, and there are Capital Ring links with Crouch Hill and Finsbury Park Stations. The finish is 100 yards from Stoke Newington Station. Highgate, Crouch Hill and Stroud Green are in Travelcard and Bus Zone 3. Finsbury Park and Lordship Park to Stoke Newington are in Zone 2, but Finsbury Park is in Zone 3 for buses coming from the north. Manor House is in both Zones 2 and 3.

**Surface and terrain**. The first 150 yards are on a very steep earth path, but this can be avoided. After that, the route is almost completely level, but the Parkland Walk has an uneven surface for nearly 2 miles, which may be muddy in places. From Finsbury Park onwards the route is on tarmac or paving. There is an avoidable flight of seven steps at Abney Park Cemetery.

**Refreshments**: Highgate, Crouch End, Stroud Green, Finsbury Park, Manor House, Woodberry Down, Clissold Park and Stoke Newington.

**Toilets**: Highgate, Finsbury Park, Clissold Park and Abney Park Cemetery.

*Capital Ring link from Highgate Station. From the ticket barriers, turn left out of the station **A** into Priory Gardens and keep ahead along the right-hand pavement for 120 yards to the footpath between house numbers 63 and 65. You join the Capital Ring here. Walk 11 comes up Priory Gardens in the opposite direction.*

Walk 12 starts from Priory Gardens, in the London Borough of Haringey, by climbing the narrow, steep earth footpath between house numbers 63 and 65 **B**. *This can be avoided by going to the station car-park exit and up to the junction of Shepherd's Hill and Archway Road **C**, or use the escalator to Archway Road **D** and turn left for 150 yards down to the same point.*

Using the footpath from Priory Gardens, take the left fork to reach Shepherd's Hill beside Highgate Library. Turn right to the junction with Archway Road **C**. Ahead lies a red-brick building, attractively festooned with ivy. Previously Highgate Methodist Church, it is now Jackson's Lane Community Centre **1**, with a theatre, café and toilets. Turn left at the lights and go down Archway Road for 50 yards to the next junction, by the Shepherds pub. From here, or from just a few yards ahead, you can see the Archway **2**, after which this road is named. Archway Road is in effect a bypass for Highgate village, which lies up Southwood Lane, on your right. It was built to avoid the very steep Highgate Hill and was

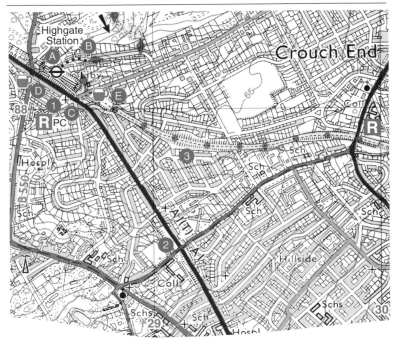

to have gone through a tunnel, but this collapsed during construction in 1812 to leave a huge chasm with no crossing point. A brick bridge provided the initial remedy, and this was replaced in 1900 by the graceful iron structure now known as the Archway.

Turn left down Holmesdale Road and follow it round to the right, then at the next bend turn left through a gate **E** into the Parkland Walk **3**. To your left is the end of a disused tunnel, once used by trains. The Capital Ring turns right, following the gradually descending former railway line for nearly 2 miles. The track is unevenly surfaced and can be muddy in places. The Parkland Walk began life as a branch of the Great Northern Railway, opened in 1867 from Finsbury Park to Edgware, with a branch to Alexandra Palace added in 1873, but it was never very successful. During the 1930s, work started on electrifying the route as a branch of the Northern Line, but World War II got in the way and the plan was abandoned. The line closed to passenger traffic in 1954, and to other traffic in 1970, then the track was eventually acquired by the London Borough of Haringey. Despite a threat to build a motorway, in 1984 the Parkland Walk became London's longest linear park, and later a nature reserve, providing a haven for wildlife in a densely populated area.

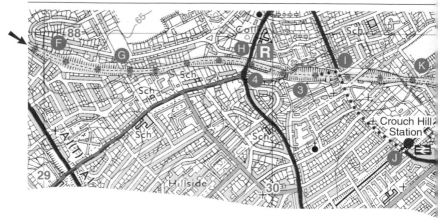

The first part of the Parkland Walk follows an embankment over Northwood Road **F** and Stanhope Road **G**. It continues through a cutting, passing under Crouch End Hill **H**. A path to the left before this leads up to Crescent Road, then immediately afterwards are the platforms of the abandoned Crouch End Station **4**. You can walk along them, or sit and rest, imagining the trains and passengers of yore. The Parkland Walk now passes under a footbridge, which marks the start of a short stretch of about 600 yards in the London Borough of Islington, passing the skateboard ramp and playground of Crouch Hill Community Centre. There is access to Crouch Hill **I** via a paved path to your left.

***Capital Ring link with Crouch Hill Station*** *(0.3 miles / 0.4 km). Take the path up to Crouch Hill, then turn right for 400 yards downhill, using the zebra crossing to continue on the opposite side to Crouch Hill Station **J**. If starting here, turn right uphill for 400 yards, using the zebra crossing to continue on the opposite side. At the top, just after the bridge, turn left down the paved path **I** and turn left again at the foot.*

The Parkland Walk continues in a cutting under Crouch Hill and Mountview Road, now back in Haringey borough, then passes a tree trail to reach another embankment across Mount Pleasant **K**. To your left is a grass-covered reservoir, while to your right in the distance can be seen high-rise blocks in East London. Another cutting leads to Stapleton Hall Road **L** in Stroud Green, where you find yourself on the topmost of three levels of transport, with the road below and the Gospel Oak to Barking railway line beneath that. This was the site of Stroud Green Station, though there is virtually nothing left of it. The route continues beside Florence Road, still in the long cutting, then bears right, crossing over Upper Tollington Park **M**. A little white tower that appears to your right, with a wind vane, sits atop Stroud Green Primary School. At the end of the Parkland Walk, bear left over a footbridge **N** into Finsbury

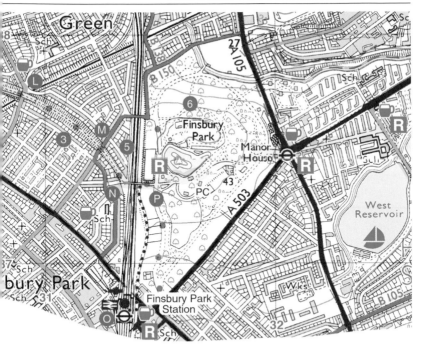

Park. Below it runs the main East Coast Main Line **5** from London to Scotland, which opened in 1850 for the Great Northern Railway and was incorporated into the London & North Eastern Railway system in 1923. Finsbury Park **6**, one of the largest open spaces in North London, developed around the old Hornsey Wood. It opened in 1862 as a replacement for the pleasure grounds taken from the people of Finsbury, a more central part of London.

*Capital Ring link with Finsbury Park Station* (0.4 miles / 0.6 km). *This follows the Parkland Walk Extension. Immediately after the footbridge **N**, inside Finsbury Park, turn right beside a fence, parallel with the railway line. Shortly turn right again to follow the enclosed path for 500 yards to Stroud Green Road. Turn left for 40 yards to the traffic lights, then cross over to Finsbury Park bus and train stations **O**. If starting here, using the Station Place exit, turn left into the bus station, then turn right to cross at the traffic lights to the Rowans leisure centre on the far side of Stroud Green Road. Turn left for 40 yards, then turn right through a gate in a high brick wall into the Parkland Walk Extension. Follow this for 500 yards to the footbridge **N**, then turn right to join the Capital Ring. N.B. At the time of writing, the Parkland Walk Extension was closed for refurbishment, expected to reopen in late 2002. If it is closed, the alternative is to follow the parallel park road down to Seven Sisters Road and turn right and right again for Station Place.*

Keep ahead across the park road **P**. In 50 yards turn left past the verandah of the park café, then turn right beside the lake. Pass a playground, then soon after the flagpole **Q** turn half-right along a path with toilets to your right. Turn left through an area with flowerbeds. At a five-way path junction, keep ahead on the path bending right and follow this past a lion-topped memorial to local campaigner Helena Fedorowicz. Keep ahead to the next junction, then turn right to cross the service road and leave the park through the main gate at the junction of A105 Green Lanes and A503 Seven Sisters Road **R**. An entrance to Manor House Station is around to the left and there are several bus stops nearby. Opposite is the Manor House pub: the manor house that gave its name to both pub and station was Hornsey Wood House, inside what is now Finsbury Park.

Green Lanes **7** originally consisted of several separate lanes that linked a series of village greens, hence the unusual plural form of the name. At nearly 7 miles, this former cattle drovers' route is now one of the longest roads in London, leading from Winchmore Hill to Newington Green. Cross over at the traffic lights towards the pub, entering as you do so the London Borough of Hackney. Before the last section of the crossing, turn right across Seven Sisters Road towards an optician's shop, where you turn left. *Alternatively you can use the station subway to the Seven Sisters Road East (south side) exit and keep ahead from the steps.* At the end of a row of shops, bear slightly right along Woodberry Down **S**. This rather bland street gives its name to the largest council housing estate in Britain **8**, comprising over 50 blocks of flats. To your left now is St Olave's **9**, the estate's parish church, dedicated to Olav Haraldsson, the 11th-century Viking king and saint.

At the end of the street, turn right along Lordship Road **T**. You soon cross the New River **10**, with its bright-green gate and signpost for the New River Path. Immediately beyond it are the Stoke Newington East and West Reservoirs **11**. The New River is neither new nor a river. It is an unnavigable artificial watercourse, completed in 1613 to bring fresh water to London from springs near Ware in Hertfordshire. To achieve this, Sir Hugh Myddelton, the Welsh engineer, devised an ingenious course that closely followed the contours of the land, dropping about 2 inches every mile, so that gravity draws the water along. The 40 miles followed by this twisting route was almost twice as far as a flight by the proverbial crow. Boosted from additional sources en route, the water flows at a rate of 40 million gallons a day, but nowadays only as far as the Stoke Newington Reservoirs here. Until recently, there was no access to the grassy banks, but the New River Path now follows them where possible all the way to Hertfordshire.

The short stretch between the reservoirs may be swarming with little flying biting beasties, so you may wish to prepare with insect repellant — or just take a deep breath and run. Continue ahead, now in Lordship Road. A little to the right rises the handsome spire of St Mary's Church in Stoke Newington, which you will pass later. In 150 yards cross a road called Queen Elizabeth's Walk **U**, then turn right along its left-hand pavement. Turn left at the junction with Allerton Road, still in Queen Elizabeth's Walk. Cross B105 Lordship Park **V** by the zebra crossing, then keep ahead, still in Queen Elizabeth's Walk. Cross to the right-hand pavement, then, opposite the Adath Yisroel Synagogue, turn right through a gate **W** into Clissold Park **12**. The park is named after the Reverend Augustus Clissold, a local parson, who during the 19th century courted his beloved, Eliza Crawshay, against the will of her father, who hated parsons and owned the local mansion, then known as Paradise House. They courted in secret, but were only able to marry after the demise of Mr Crawshay, and promptly renamed the mansion Clissold House.

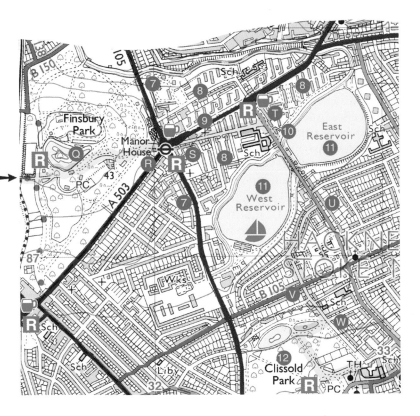

The two small lakes ahead were formed by damming Hackney Brook, and are named after the park's founders. Keep ahead along the left bank of the first, Runtzmere. Just before the second, Beckmere **X**, turn sharp left along an avenue of turkey-oak and horse-chestnut trees. At the far end, you pass between a playground, an open-air stage and a toilet block to reach the back of Clissold House **13**, with the magnificent spire of St Mary's Church **14** soaring ahead. The house contains the park ranger's office and (at the front) a café. An intriguing inscription above a functioning water fountain here appears to indicate that it is in memory of the three daughters of Wilson Yeates Esq., aged 134 years, but on closer inspection it becomes clear that, sadly, the sisters died at the ages of one, three and four. Turn left before the house, past the playground, and fork left, with the spire now to your right. The smaller Ancient Mother Church **15** appears on your right, after which you turn right through a gate **Y** and follow a fenced footpath through the graveyard. Turn left at Stoke Newington Church Street.

During the 17th and 18th centuries, the village of Stoke Newington became a refuge for dissenters and nonconformists excluded from the City of London. One of these was Daniel Defoe (1660 – 1731), writer, political activist and secret agent, who lived in Church Street and is of course most famous for *Robinson Crusoe* and *Moll Flanders*. His name lives on in the names of a street, a school and a pub. The two parish churches of Stoke Newington face each other across Church Street. The older and smaller of the two, built in 1563, is the old St Mary's, now called the Ancient Mother Church. The larger and more imposing one opposite, with its 220-foot spire, is the new St Mary's, designed by George Gilbert Scott and consecrated in 1858.

At just under 4 miles (6.4 km) from Charing Cross, this is as close as the Capital Ring gets to central London. Keep ahead along the left-hand pavement of Church Street, with the former Stoke Newington Town Hall **16** ahead. You pass Stoke Newington Library **17**, where Daniel Defoe's tombstone is displayed. Soon after the Daniel Defoe pub, turn left through a small gate **Z** and climb seven steps into Abney Park Cemetery **18**. *The steps can be avoided by continuing ahead to the High Street **AA**, then turning left for a few yards to the main gates of the cemetery.* Abney Park Cemetery is a cheerfully eerie place, whose 300,000 graves are framed by foliage amid an air of controlled abandonment. It is owned by the London Borough of Hackney, which has set up a trust to prevent further decay without spoiling the habitats that have made this an official nature reserve. The cemetery was laid out in 1840 but never consecrated, enabling the many religious dissenters that lived in this area to be buried here.

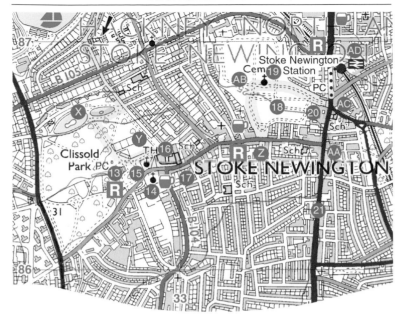

Inside the cemetery, keep ahead along a narrow path between graves, then at the main path turn left. Almost opposite is the tomb of William Booth (1829 – 1912), founder of the Salvation Army, and his wife, Catherine, while next to it are buried several other early Salvation Army luminaries. Keep to the main path as it bears right to an intersection **AB**, where you turn right to pass the derelict chapel **19** at the centre of the cemetery. A short distance to the right is a Commonwealth War Memorial, which provides a good view of the chapel, and beyond that the grave of and memorial to Isaac Watts, the 18th-century nonconformist preacher and hymn-writer. Keep ahead, passing a sundial set into a brick circle, towards the main gate into Stoke Newington High Street. The cemetery's visitor centre is located in the lodge **20** on your right, and toilets in the on one your left. A plaque set in the ground between them bears Egyptian hieroglyphics and their translation: 'The great gate of the mortal part of man'.

Pass through the main gate, then turn left along A10 Stamford Hill. Cross at the lights to the junction with Cazenove Road **AC**, where Walk 12 ends. The dead-straight A10, or Great Cambridge Road, follows the line of Ermine Street **21**, the Roman road from Chichester through London to York. *To continue to Walk 13, keep ahead along Cazenove Road. Stoke Newington Station **AD** is 100 yards to the left up Stamford Hill, with bus stops nearby.*

*The magnificent spire of St Mary's Church in Stoke Newington soars 220 feet abou*

*Clissold Park. Its older sister church lies behind the trees on the left.*

# 13 STOKE NEWINGTON TO HACKNEY WICK

**Distance**: 3.6 miles (5.9 km). Excludes Capital Ring links of 0.1 miles (0.1 km) from Stoke Newington Station and 0.3 miles (0.5 km) to Hackney Wick Station.

**Public transport**. The start of Walk 13 is 100 yards from Stoke Newington Station and close to bus stops. There is a Capital Ring link with Clapton Station. It finishes on a bus route and 500 yards from Hackney Wick Station. All places on this walk are in Travelcard and Bus Zone 2, except Lea Bridge Road in Zone 3. Clapton Station is in both Zones 2 and 3.

**Surface and terrain**. The route is almost entirely level, but in Springfield Park there is a short and fairly steep descent including a flight of steps (avoidable via a diversion). There are some very short but quite steep ascents and descents on the Lee Navigation towpath. Most of the route is on tarmac or paving, but much of the Lee Navigation towpath has an uneven surface and may be muddy in places.

**Refreshments**: Stoke Newington, Springfield Park, Lea Bridge Road and Hackney Wick.

**Toilets**: Springfield Park.

*Capital Ring link from Stoke Newington Station and buses. From the station exit **A**, turn left along Stamford Hill for 100 yards past some of the station bus stops to the junction with Cazenove Road **B**. You join the Capital Ring by turning left here.*

Walk 13 starts at the junction of Stamford Hill and Cazenove Road **B** in the London Borough of Hackney. Keep ahead along Cazenove Road, which is lined with magnificent centenarian plane trees, planted soon after 1900. In 300 yards you cross Alkham Road, then pass a green-domed building **1** on your right, actually a mosque that has been rather cleverly converted from several Victorian terrace houses. It is properly called Stamford Hill Masjid-e-Quba, named after the first mosque built by the Prophet Mohammed.

Take the next left, Kyverdale Road **C**, cross over and in 80 yards turn right along Filey Avenue **D**, following it all the way to the main road, past Jubilee Primary School and across Chardmore Road **E**. At A107 Clapton Common **F**, turn left and go over the zebra crossing, then turn right and immediately left along Springfield. In 100 yards keep ahead through the gate **G** into Springfield Park **2**.

Bear left past the lake, with the 19th-century Springfield House **3** on your left, *which has toilets (in the lobby) and a weekend café*. Pass between

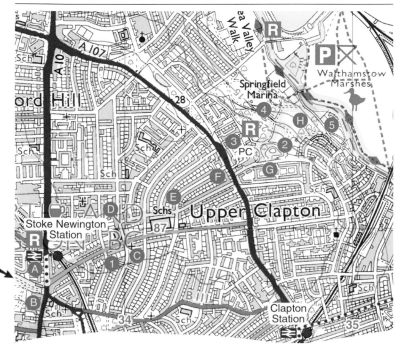

some bollards, turn right, then bear left downhill on a tarmac path. Ahead of you now is a good view across the Lea Valley towards Walthamstow. At a path junction, you pass 'the two giants of Springfield Park' **4**: two tall beech trees, as commemorated in a poem in the lobby of Springfield House. Continue ahead, descending more steeply, down seven steps, along a path that bears right past tennis courts. *To avoid the steps, you can turn right at the 'two giants' and follow paths down the right-hand side of the park, though this is still steep.* At the next junction, turn right to leave the park through a gate **H**, then turn left past a barrier along a fenced tarmac path beside the Lee Navigation **5**. For centuries, the Lea formed the boundary between Essex and Middlesex, before the existence of Greater London, and now performs the same task between the London Boroughs of Hackney and Waltham Forest. For just as long, its spelling has caused many an argument. An early form was Ley, but Acts of Parliament insist on Lee, and Lea is how it appears on many maps. An informal compromise has been reached whereby creations, such as the navigation and the regional park, are Lee, while natural manifestations, such as the river itself and the valley, are Lea. The river flows from the Chiltern Hills near Luton to the Thames at Bow Creek, and has provided a major route of communication since prehistoric times. The Lea Valley Walk follows the river for 50 miles from near Luton to Bow Locks, and the Capital Ring joins it for the next 3 miles.

In 80 yards turn sharp right up a short but steep ramp to cross Horseshoe Bridge **I**, another typical canal crossover bridge, entering the London Borough of Waltham Forest. This stretch of the route is half green, that is, generally green on one side and built up on the other, with residential or commercial buildings. The skyline is sometimes dominated by power cables and pylons, but there is enough interest elsewhere to take your mind off them. To your left is Springfield Marina **6**, full of colourful narrowboats, which occupies the Coppermill Stream, a branch of the Lea. On the far side of the bridge, turn right, going steeply down, and keep ahead along a dirt track parallel to the towpath, with some picnic tables nearby. A broad ditch separates you from Walthamstow Marsh Nature Reserve **7**, one of the few remaining areas of natural wetland in Greater London, where the dominant vegetation is sedge and reeds.

Away to the left, among high-rise blocks, soars the spire of St Saviour's, the parish church of Walthamstow. The view ahead is dominated by a viaduct through Clapton Junction **8**, which carries commuter trains and the Stansted Airport express services. It was in some of these arches that the aviator A.V. Roe constructed his early aeroplanes at the beginning of the 20th century. They were tested with flights across the marshes, which provided a mercifully soft surface for the many crash landings. Just before the railway bridge, the little Anchor & Hope pub **9** is tantalisingly out of reach on the opposite bank — the High Hill Ferry that operated here ceased in the 1950s. The adjacent red-brick building was once the Beehive pub. Beyond the bridge, the track rises a little to reveal a huge bubble ahead: it is the Lea Valley Ice Centre **10**, attracting skaters all year round. As you approach it, where the river bends right, bear right at a signpost and descend steps or ramp to cross the footbridge **J**, returning to Hackney borough.

**Capital Ring link with Clapton Station** *(0.4 miles / 0.7 km). As the river swings left, at North Millfields Recreation Ground **K**, turn right, following the arrow in the ground-set plaque, along a paved path, then keep ahead up Southwold Road to Upper Clapton Road, where you turn left to Clapton Station **L**. If starting here, turn right out of the station exit. In 30 yards turn right again down Southwold Road all the way to North Millfields Recreation Ground **K** and the Lee Navigation, where you turn right along the towpath.*

Continuing beside the Lee Navigation, you come to Lea Bridge **M**, carrying the very busy Lea Bridge Road. Pass under the bridge, then, with the terrace of the Princess of Wales pub on your right, the river and navigation separate for a while: the Old River Lea flows off to the left, while the Lee Navigation continues ahead. Soon afterwards, you cross Curtain Gate Bridge **N** and stay on the east bank for the rest of Walk 13. Behind a long brick wall lie the former Middlesex Filter Beds **11**, now a nature reserve. *It is worth going inside the gate and immediately turning left through a second gate to see the 'Ackney 'Enge – Hackney's version of Stonehenge – which formed the base for a pumping engine.* The filter beds occupy the north end of Hackney Marsh **12**, on an island formed by the river and navigation. At the end of the wall is a pavilion, behind which stretches a vast sea of over 80 football pitches. When trees are bare, you can see a large building beyond, which is New Spitalfields Market, moved here from central London in 1991.

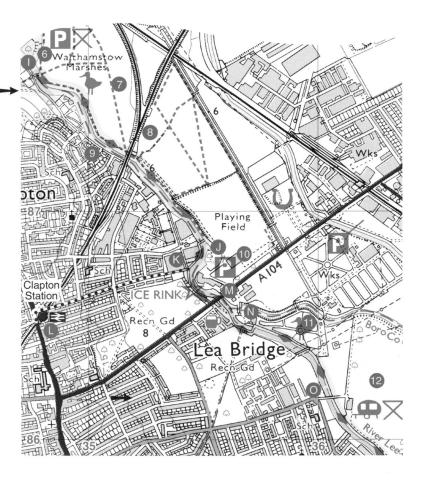

The towpath now becomes more uneven and narrow, and may be muddy and puddly in places. There are some narrow squeeze-stiles, which pushchairs and wheelchairs would have to be lifted over, or there is a parallel tarmac track to the left. Ahead in the distance, the tops of the tallest buildings at Canary Wharf can be seen. Soon after a right-hand bend, you reach Cow Bridge **O**. The red-brick building with ornate gables is Mandeville Primary School, opened in 1902. Left- and right-hand bends lead to Marshgate Bridge **P**, carrying B112 Homerton Road. Immediately before the bridge, on the far bank, is the former Lesney works **13**, famed for its Matchbox toys and still proudly displaying the company name, though the building's future is uncertain.

Continue along the towpath, still narrow and uneven, under the bridge. To your left now is Wick Field Recreation Ground, while ahead looms the bridge of the A102M motorway, which has taken most of the traffic away from the old Eastway Bridge **Q** beyond. Behind Arena Field Recreation Ground to your left rise the mournful grey stands of Hackney Greyhound Stadium **14**, though no doubt they come to life during meetings. To the right of a derelict covered-concrete foot-bridge rise the twin windvane-topped towers of Gainsborough Primary School. The towpath passes through an industrial area, below

*At the north end of Hackney Marsh lies the 'Ackney 'Enge – all that remains of a pumping station in the former Middlesex Filter Beds.*

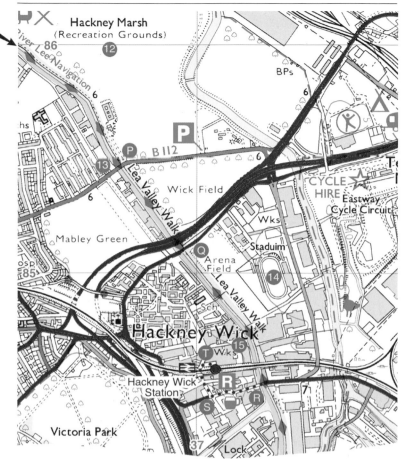

which runs the Channel Tunnel Rail Link. Nestling into the far bank is the little Johnstone Boat House **15**, built in 1934 and now the home of Eton Mission Rowing Club. Finally, you pass under a railway bridge carrying the North London Line to reach Carpenters Road Bridge **R**, where Walk 13 ends, just across the boundary with the London Borough of Tower Hamlets. *Walk 14 continues along the towpath.*

***Capital Ring link to Hackney Wick Station*** *(0.3 miles / 0.5 km). Go under the bridge **R** and turn sharp left up a steep, cobbled ramp to A115 Carpenters Road. Turn left across the bridge, where the road becomes White Post Lane. Keep to the left-hand pavement past a bus stop and the Lea Tavern, continuing around the bend for 100 yards to a zebra crossing **S**. Turn right here along Hepscott Road and keep ahead under the bridge in Wallis Road to find the entrance to Hackney Wick Station **T** on your right.*

*The Greenway, seen here near Plaistow, was laid out on top of sewage pipes runni*

*...rom Hackney to Beckton (Walk 14).*

# 14 HACKNEY WICK TO BECKTON DISTRICT PARK

**Distance**: 4.6 miles (7.5 km). Excludes Capital Ring links of 0.3 miles (0.5 km) from Hackney Wick Station and 0.2 miles (0.3 km) to Royal Albert Station.

**Public transport.** The start of Walk 14 is on a bus route and 500 yards from Hackney Wick Station. There are Capital Ring links en route with Pudding Mill Lane and West Ham Stations. The finish in Beckton District Park is on a bus route and 350 yards from Royal Albert Station (Docklands Light Railway). All places on this walk are in Travelcard and Bus Zone 3, except Hackney Wick and Fish Island in Zone 2. Pudding Mill Lane Station is in both Zones 2 and 3.

**Surface and terrain.** Almost the entire route is on a hard surface, consisting of paving, tarmac or bonded gravel. The only exception is the first half-mile on a rough and narrow towpath, which may be wet and muddy at times. Nearly all the walk is level, but there are some short and fairly steep slopes. Access to The Greenway is by flights of steps, with alternative ramps. The Greenway is a permissive path, which is closed at night.

**Refreshments**: Hackney Wick, Plaistow and Beckton District Park.

**Toilets**: Plaistow and Beckton District Park.

*Capital Ring link with Hackney Wick Station (0.3 miles / 0.5 km). From the station exit **A**, turn left under the bridge, then bear left along Hepscott Road, passing the station bus stops. Cross White Post Lane and keep ahead to A115 Rothbury Road **B**. Go over the zebra crossing and turn left. Keep ahead past the Lea Tavern, now in White Post Lane again, and rise to the canal bridge. Ignore the towpath to the right before the bridge – this leads on to the Hertford Union Canal. Cross the bridge **C**, turn right through a gate and descend the steep cobbled ramp. You join the Capital Ring here. Walk 13 of the Capital Ring comes in from behind, under the bridge.*

*The towpath section and the restriction at Old Ford can be avoided by joining The Greenway at its start in Wick Lane **E** and following it for 250 yards eastwards to the bridge over the Lee Navigation **D**, where the Capital Ring comes up to The Greenway.*

Walk 14 starts at Carpenters Road Bridge **C** in the London Borough of Tower Hamlets. Keep ahead along the east (left) bank of the Lee Navigation, with the tall buildings of Canary Wharf far ahead. Opposite is the entrance to the Hertford Union Canal **1**, also known as Duckett's Cut after its promoter, Sir George Duckett, who got the canal through to completion in 1830. You can see the first of three locks that take the canal up past Victoria Park and on to the Regent's Canal at Bow Wharf. The area to the left of the canal entrance is known as Fish Island **2**, where some streets have fishy names. It was once notorious for foul-smelling industries, whose effluents polluted

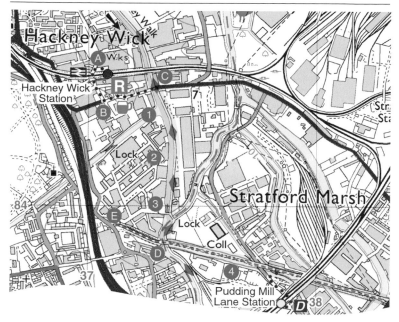

the river and canal, but they have closed down and a regeneration scheme is turning the district into a burgeoning business area.

The towpath rises at several points with rails leading off to the left — they are the remnants of crane tracks used for loading barges in the days when goods were largely transported on water. In 500 yards you reach the twin Old Ford Locks **3**. The adjacent building, once the lockkeeper's cottage, houses the studios of television production company Planet 24 and was the location for Channel 4's *Big Breakfast* until its demise in 2002. Continue ahead over a footbridge, where the Old River Lea rejoins the Navigation, and you enter the London Borough of Newham for the rest of Walk 14. Turn right down the ramp, where restricted space would require pushchairs and wheelchairs to be lifted over. The Roman road from London to Colchester crossed the Lea hereabouts and remained in use until the early 12th century, hence the name Old Ford. It is believed to have been closed after Queen Maud, wife of Henry I, was unceremoniously, and presumably accidentally, ducked into the river, and she commanded a new road to be built further south, now Stratford High Street.

In a few more yards you reach an overhead bridge **D**, where you part company with the Lea Valley Walk. Immediately after the bridge, turn left through a barrier and go up a tarmac ramp to join a long embankment known as The Greenway **4**. The Greenway is a most imaginative use of sewage pipes: a level trackway of bonded gravel for walkers and cyclists laid on top of the Northern Outfall Sewage Embankment — the acronym, NOSE, may have been deliberately chosen by an engineer with a sense of humour. The embankment runs for nearly 6 miles (9.6 km) from Hackney to Beckton, where the sewage is treated before discharge into the Thames. It is part of the extensive sewerage system designed for London in the 1860s by Sir Joseph Bazalgette, most of which still functions today. With four 9-inch pipes, the Northern Outfall is thought to contain the biggest sewage flow in Britain at over 100 million gallons a day. For the next 3 miles, with just two short diversions, the Capital Ring follows this hidden green marvel through an otherwise rather bland part of London that consists mostly of residential and commercial districts.

Turn right along the embankment. To your left now is the Old Ford Nature Reserve. From your elevated position on top of the embankment, you have a grandstand view, dominated by Canary Wharf to your right. A line of willow trees to your left signals the approach of Pudding Mill River **5**. It used to continue to the right but has been cut short and is now rather stagnant. Pudding Mill River is one of several channels, known collectively as the Bow Back Rivers, that have been cut by the River Lea through this once marshy area. The Capital Ring encounters four of them. They are tidal and mostly navigable, though nowadays little used. At low tide there are rich pickings in the mud for birds, and you may see the blue flash of a kingfisher. Cross Pudding Mill Lane, then a broad swathe of very busy railway tracks lies ahead. It is one of only two obstacles through which The Greenway cannot pass, so you must briefly come off it by bearing right down a ramp **F** 100 yards before the railway.

*Capital Ring link to Pudding Mill Lane DLR Station (0.2 miles / 0.3 km). Instead of using the ramp, descend the steps F to an area that was being redeveloped at the time of writing. A temporary route turns right, back under The Greenway bridge to Pudding Mill Lane. Turn sharp left for 150 yards under the railway bridge to find Pudding Mill Lane DLR Station G on your right. If starting here, turn left from the station exit and pass under the railway bridge. In 150 yards go under The Greenway bridge and turn sharp right along a path, back under the bridge. Shortly on your left, climb 32 steps F up to The Greenway, where you turn right – only to come off it again as described above.*

At the foot of the ramp, go ahead under the railway through a short tunnel, part of Marshgate Lane. This is currently the most forbidding part of the whole Capital Ring, among fly-tips and grim scrapyards, though improvements are planned. The bridge carries the main line from Liverpool Street to East Anglia **6** and the Docklands

Light Railway's Stratford branch. The line was opened in 1839 for the Eastern Counties Railway and later absorbed by the Great Eastern Railway. On leaving the tunnel past a gate, immediately turn left along an enclosed earth path. At the end, ascend the steps or ramp and turn right to continue along The Greenway, where you are welcomed back by a jolly blue metal banner surmounted by a procession of metal people.

Straightaway you cross two more Bow Back Rivers — City Mill **7**, then Waterworks **8** — to reach the second diversion, the very busy A11 Stratford High Street **H**. Do not attempt to cross the road here: turn right for 100 yards to cross at the traffic lights beside Abbey Lane **I**, then turn left along the far side to rejoin The Greenway. The left-hand side is now occupied by industry and warehousing, so looking to your right is a better bet, despite the row of pylons marching alongside the path. After passing Abbey Lane Open Space **9**, you glimpse the shimmering, onion-shaped roof of Thames Water's new, award-winning Abbey Mills Pumping Station **10**, opened in 1997. On the bridge **11** over Abbey Lane, you cross the Meridian Line again. It used to be marked by coloured stones, crossing at an angle, and others featuring a rocket blasting towards a group of planets. The stones have been removed, but lighter patches betray their shapes.

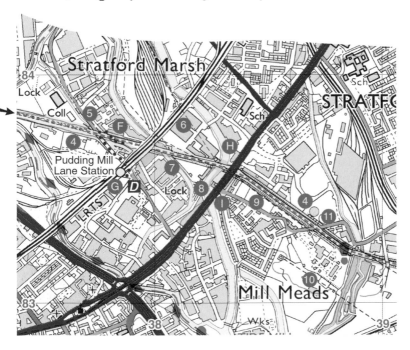

Appearing now through the trees is the eccentric old Abbey Mills Pumping Station **12**, looking like an oriental palace. The Grade II listed Victorian building, opened in 1868, was another part of Sir Joseph Bazalgette's immense scheme for ridding London of its sewage. With its cupola and gilded spire, and an interior like a Byzantine church, it suffered the soubriquet 'The Temple of Sewage' during its working life. Just past the old pumping station, to your right, is a curious metal object **13**, shaped like a giant ammonite shellfish. Installed in 1914, but no longer used, it pumped away storm water in times of heavy rainfall. The pump lies beside the last and widest of the Bow Back Rivers, Channelsea **14**. Looking right as you cross, it splits into two, with Abbey Creek flowing to the right and Channelsea Creek to the left. The area to your left after the river was the site of Stratford Langthorne Abbey, from which this area takes its name. You cross Canning Road at surface level, then one high-sided concrete bridge takes you over the Jubilee Line **15**, extended to Stratford in 2000, and another leads over Manor Road **J**.

*This jolly metal banner welcomes you back to The Greenway at Stratford – a cheerful sight after the grim scrapyards on Marshgate Lane.*

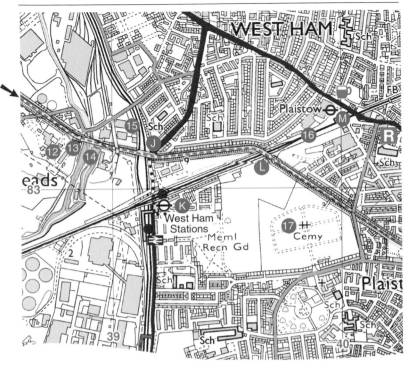

***Capital Ring link to West Ham Station*** *(0.2 miles / 0.3 km). Immediately after crossing Manor Road* **J***, take the steps down to the right and turn right (or use the ramp a few yards further on), then turn left along Manor Road. Continue along Manor Road for 250 yards, pass under the bridges, then turn left along Memorial Avenue to West Ham Station* **K***. If starting here, turn right from the station exit then right again under the bridges. Walk along Manor Road for 250 yards, crossing Alan Hocken Way. Just before the next bridge, turn right then immediately left up 31 steps* **J***, or keep ahead up the ramp, turning right at the top along The Greenway.*

Ranelagh Primary School rises to the left behind houses, then The Greenway makes a sharp turn to the right, crossing the District Line and the London to Southend Railway **16**. *Just beyond this is an access point* **L** *signed Plaistow Station* **M***, 500 yards away to your left – this is not a Capital Ring link, but you can reach it fairly easily by keeping close to the railway line.* You pass the Memorial Recreation Ground to your right, then the East London Cemetery **17**. Among those buried here is the World War I German spy, Carl Hans Lody, one of the last people to be executed at the Tower of London in 1914. Although he had been working for the enemy, he was much admired for the brave and dignified manner in which he met his end.

*The old Abbey Mills Pumping Station, operating from 1868 to 1997, was known as 'The Temple of Sewage'.*

The Greenway comes to Upper Road **N**, the first of four busy roads in Plaistow which you cross in quick succession at surface level, via traffic lights. Approaching Balaam Street **O**, to your right rise the twin domed towers of Plaistow Memorial Baptist Church **18**, a majestic red-brick building opened in 1921. At Barking Road **P** is the grey-stone St Andrew's Church **19**, built in 1870, with its similar adjacent vicarage. After lying derelict for more than a decade, it found a new lease of life in 1985 as an independent multicultural church. Prince Regent Lane **Q** soon follows. *There is an automatic toilet to the left along both of these last two roads, near the point where they converge.* Beyond Prince Regent Lane, Newham General Hospital **20** spreads for several hundred yards along the right-hand side.

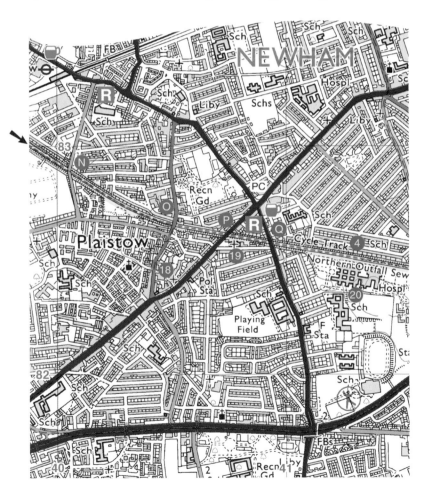

Fourteen large concrete balls mark Boundary Lane **R**. Beyond that, with Brampton Manor School **21** on your right, you can see ahead the huge Barking Creek Flood Barrier, nearly 3 miles (5 km) away. Completed in 1982, it towers 193 feet (58 metres) above the mouth of the River Roding and the Thames.

Soon after the end of the school playground, between two metal banners, you take your leave of The Greenway by turning right down steps or ramp **S**. Keep ahead along Stokes Road, then turn left along the misleadingly named Roman Road **T**, which is not Roman at all — it commemorates the discovery of Roman burials nearby in 1863, during gravel extraction for the NOSE. In 50 yards turn right into Noel Road **U** to reach A13 Newham Way **V**, which you cross on a footbridge with steps and ramps. Look left to see 'Beckton Alps': the giant slagheap of a former gasworks, grassed over and converted into a dry ski slope. On the far side, continue in the same direction along a street called Viking Gardens. To reach this you cross Jack Dash Way, named after the dockers' union leader who frequently hit the headlines in the 1950s and 1960s.

At the end of the street, continue ahead through a gate **W** into Beckton District Park **22**. On top of an apartment building to the left, note the wind vane depicting a ship and crane, another reminder of the dockworking background of this area.

The remainder of Walk 14 winds through this very pleasant park, bending first right then left along the main path. Ignore side turnings, but note that the right-hand side of the main path is a cycle track. The winding path is part of a tree trail, with marker plates describing the wide variety of unusual trees from all over the world. On reaching the first of several trim-trail fixtures, it is worth making a short diversion to the right to see the pretty lake **23** and its waterbirds. *The building at the far end has toilets and a seasonal refreshment kiosk.*

Cross Tollgate Road **X** at the refuge and continue through the park, bearing left then right past houses. The path winds around a meadow, which is being managed to encourage wild flowers. Keep ahead past the Will Thorne Pavilion **24** and a playground, with Stansfeld Road to your right. Walk 14 ends at the next path junction **Y**. *To continue on to Walk 15, turn left here.*

***Capital Ring link to Royal Albert DLR Station*** *(0.2 miles / 0.3 km). Turn right at the path junction **Y** and cross Stansfeld Road at the zebra crossing. Turn left for 150 yards to a roundabout at the junction with A1020 Royal Albert Way **Z**, passing the Strait Road bus stops. Bear right to cross the dual carriageway at the lights, then keep ahead along the fenced tarmac path to Royal Albert Station **AA** on the Docklands Light Railway.*

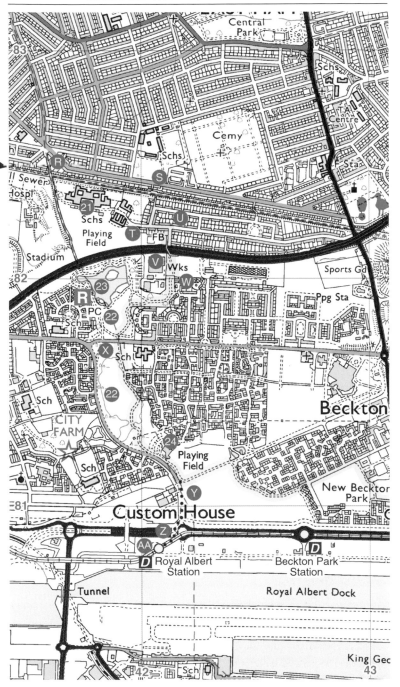

# 15 BECKTON DISTRICT PARK TO WOOLWICH

**Distance**: 3.3 miles (5.4 km). Excludes Capital Ring links 0.2 miles (0.3 km) from Royal Albert Station and 0.6 miles (0.9 km) to Woolwich Arsenal Station.

**Public transport**. The start of Walk 15 is on a bus route and 350 yards from Royal Albert Station. The route passes Cyprus and Gallions Reach Stations, and North Woolwich Station. The finish is 100 yards from several bus routes and the Woolwich Free Ferry, and half a mile from Woolwich Arsenal Station. All places on this walk are in Travelcard and Bus Zone 3, except Woolwich Arsenal in Zone 4. Buses at Beckton Park, Cyprus and Gallions Reach are in both Zones 3 and 4.

**Surface and terrain**. Almost the entire walk is on a hard surface of paving or tarmac, though there are several short stretches along uneven earth paths beside Gallions Reach. It is entirely level apart from some very short slopes. There is, however, the small matter of the Woolwich Foot Tunnel, which has over 100 steps on each side, though there are also lifts.

**Refreshments**: Cyprus, North Woolwich and Woolwich.

**Toilets**: New Beckton Park, North Woolwich and Woolwich.

*Capital Ring link from Royal Albert DLR Station (0.2 miles / 0.3 km). At the foot of the steps A from the platforms, turn back under the tracks (from the lifts keep ahead). Go through a metal gate and along a tarmac path to A1020 Royal Albert Way B. Keep ahead at the traffic lights over the dual carriageway, then turn right and bear left into Stansfeld Road, passing the Strait Road bus stops. Go over the zebra crossing to the path junction C in Beckton District Park.*

Walk 15 of the Capital Ring starts in Beckton District Park **1** at the path junction beside Stansfeld Road **C**, south of the Will Thorne Pavilion, where you are in the London Borough of Newham. It is planned that the route will eventually go southwards from here to follow the proposed promenade beside Royal Albert Dock. For the moment, the route continues through the park along a path beside a fenced trotting track, on the route of the former Beckton Railway. On the far side **D**, turn right between trees, keeping close to houses on your left, then bear left to a path junction **E**. *Beckton Park DLR Station F is just 150 yards along a path to the right here, though this is not a Capital Ring link.* The Capital Ring continues ahead between the houses. At Harper Road/Parry Avenue, keep ahead along the right-hand side of the road (Savage Gardens), beside New Beckton Park **2**. In 200 yards, opposite Oakes Close **G**, turn right along a path across the park, beside the fence of the Stroud Pavilion (*there are toilets inside*).

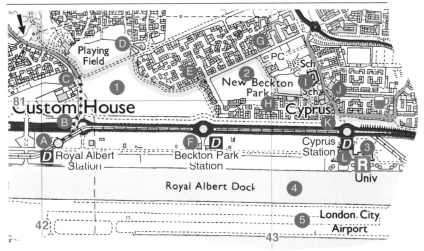

Arriving at houses **H**, turn left along a footpath beside them, passing a playground. In 125 yards you reach a grass area **I**, then bear half-right on a curving path between houses. Follow this to a cul-de-sac called Learoyd Gardens and carry on to East Ham Manor Way **J**. Turn right to a mini-roundabout and turn left via a refuge across Strait Road **K**. The Capital Ring currently continues ahead along Cyprus Place, but a short diversion is strongly recommended into the Docklands Campus of the University of East London **3**, as outlined in the next paragraph.

*After Strait Road, cross a footbridge, in between Cyprus DLR Station **L** below and Royal Albert Way above. Keep ahead past the main entrance to the side of Royal Albert Dock **4**. When the Docklands Campus of the University of East London opened in 1999, it was the first new university campus built in London for over 50 years. Appropriately, it specialises in technology and multimedia, since the buildings were designed to maximise energy efficiency and were built on recycled soil. The University was formed in 1992 from the former North East London Polytechnic, and has two other campuses, in Barking and Stratford. Student apartments with butterfly-wing roofs overlook the Royal Albert Dock, over a mile long, which opened in 1880 and linked with two others to form the Royal Docks, in their day the largest in the world. Closed to commercial shipping in 1982, they continue in use as massive watersports facilities – Royal Albert has an Olympic standard rowing course and stages regular regattas. On its far side is the runway of London City Airport **5**, opened in 1987 and fast expanding: in that year only 15,000 passengers passed through; now the annual figure is rapidly approaching the two million mark. It is hoped that the Capital Ring will eventually follow the dockside, but for the moment you must return to Cyprus Place **K** and turn right.*

*The former Gallions Hotel, framed by the columns of a DLR viaduct.*

The Cyprus estate, constructed in 1881, took its name from the British capture of the island a few years earlier. At the bend, opposite the Ferndale pub **M**, bear right along a tarmac footpath between houses and trees to reach Gallions Roundabout **N**. Turn right, using pedestrian crossings with traffic lights, and, following signs to Gallions Reach Station, cross ahead and left to the central island, with its polygonal red-brick pumping station. Turn right to go anticlockwise, crossing an access road into the pumping station. At the next set of lights, cross right then left towards the viaduct of the Docklands Light Railway **O**. *To avoid obstructions along the riverside stretch, people with wheelchairs can turn right here along Woolwich Manor Way for half a mile, then, after crossing the entrance to King George V Dock, turn left through the Galleons Lock estate to rejoin the riverside.*

Turn left below the viaduct, noting the large building ahead, standing all alone in wasteland. This was the Gallions Hotel **6**, opened in 1883, where passengers stayed before embarking on P&O liners sailing from the Royal Docks. At the time of writing, the future of this distinguished dockland relic was still to be decided. Turn right at Armada Way **P**, with Gallions Reach DLR Station **Q** opposite. In 200 yards, at a roundabout **R**, turn right into a works entrance, then turn left before the barrier along a fenced footpath, aiming for a radio mast. This leads in 400 yards to Gallions Reach **7** itself, a stretch of the River Thames. At the time of writing, you had to climb a short gravel slope **S** up to the river wall, but this should be replaced soon by something more permanent. The word 'reach' in this instance refers to an open stretch of water along a river;

originally the word was used to denote the distance that could be sailed by a vessel on one tack. Gallions Reach is named after the Galyons, a leading family in this area in the 14th century. Looking left along Barking Reach, past the dam, you can see the huge Ford motor works at Dagenham. Stretching 3 miles to the left along the south bank, beyond the riverside scrub, the comparatively new town of Thamesmead has been built on what was once the weapon testing grounds of the Royal Arsenal (see below). Looking right, you can see Shooters Hill rising to the highest point of the Capital Ring, passed on Walk 1.

Turn right along the concrete footpath beside the wall, which will eventually form part of the north-east extension of the Thames Path, from the Thames Barrier to Purfleet. Approaching Gallions Reach Marina **8**, you turn away from the river to cross the narrow gate of the entrance lock **T**, much reduced in size from its days of serving the Royal Albert Dock. On the far side lies the Royal Docks Campus of Newham College of Further Education **9**, where construction courses take place. Turn right along winding Gallions Road, then in 100 yards at a bend **U**, take care as you cross over and turn left along a fenced earth path back to the river wall. The path soon turns inland again, and you climb six steps up and down over the wall to cross the massive gates of the still-functioning lock **V** into King George V Dock **10**. In its heyday, this huge lock, measuring 800 feet long by 100 feet wide (240 by 30 metres) was capable of admitting some of the world's largest liners. If a (now much

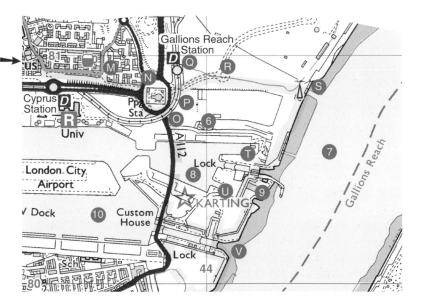

*The student apartments of the University of East London's Docklands Campus overlo*

*the Royal Albert Dock, now an Olympic standard rowing course.*

smaller) vessel is passing through, the lock area will be closed and you may have to wait a few minutes. *Or you can keep ahead to the main road, turn left and return on a path parallel to the other side of the lock.* On the far side, you climb steps over the wall again then turn sharp left onto the promenade **W** beside the Galleons Lock **11** residential development — the different spelling is intentional. On the opposite bank now lie the historic grey-stone buildings of the former Royal Arsenal **12** at Woolwich, established in 1545 to test army weaponry. It was closed in 1967 and has been gradually handed over for redevelopment. Floating on the water in front is Royal Arsenal Pier **13**, opened in 2002. You should now be able to make out journey's end, the little circular red-brick exit of the foot tunnel in Woolwich, though it is still a mile away on foot.

At the end of the promenade, turn right and down the slope into Bargehouse Road **X**, turning sharp left back to the riverside, either via a slipway or steps on the right. *At the time of writing this connection had not been made: if this is still the case, you will need to return to the centre of the promenade, turn left to Woolwich Manor Way, then turn left at the bend along Bargehouse Road.* This is the landing point of an earlier incarnation of the Woolwich Ferry. Bear right along a fenced path along the river wall. Ahead now are the terminals of the Woolwich Free Ferry and the dockyard chimney that you passed on Walk 1. The riverside path angles around another former ferry slipway, then climbs to pass through a gate **Y** into Royal Victoria Gardens **14**. Continue beside the river, noting on your right a steam hammer of 1888, rescued from a blacksmith's shop in Royal Albert Dock. At the end of the park, keep left up the fenced ramp and go through a gate to continue beside the river wall.

On reaching a derelict jetty **Z**, yet another previous ferry landing point, the route continues ahead. Or you can climb 14 steps up and down for a short cut via a refuge across Pier Road to North Woolwich Station **AA** and North Woolwich Old Station Museum **15** — take care, as this is the busy approach road to the ferry. The museum occupies the original North Woolwich Station buildings, built in 1854, and contains steam engines, old rolling stock and railway memorabilia, as well as toilets and a refreshment kiosk. Continue along the river wall almost to the ferry terminal, then bear sharp right up a ramp **AB**, with a step up at its foot. Go up and down, then turn sharp right, back along the approach road. Go over an informal zebra crossing to the circular red-brick entrance **AC** into the Woolwich Foot Tunnel **16**.

Although the Woolwich Free Ferry (see Walk 1) crosses the river parallel to the tunnel, most Capital Ring walkers will surely eschew the spartan lounges of the ferry to complete their epic journey on foot through the tunnel. However, claustrophobics may prefer the ferry. The

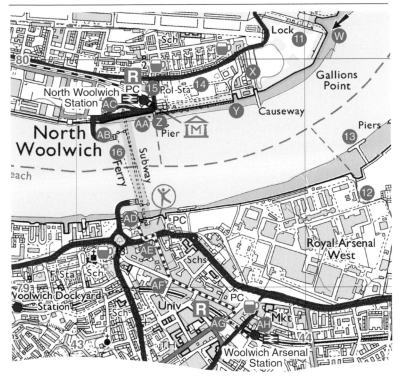

Woolwich Foot Tunnel, opened in 1912, is open 24 hours a day and is 550 yards (495 metres) long. Please note that dogs must be kept on a lead. Although there are lifts at each end, purists may wish to use the steps — 126 down on the north side, 101 up on the south side. Halfway through, you return to the London Borough of Woolwich, which shares responsibility for the tunnel with Newham. Having reached the top of the steps on the south side, head for the Capital Ring signpost **AD** and touch it to mark your completion. If there is nobody around, you may even feel inclined to give three cheers. Congratulations! Please let TfL Street Management know that you have completed the route, with dates and number of people (see Useful Addresses, page 167).

***Capital Ring link to Woolwich Arsenal Station*** *(0.6 miles / 0.9 km). From the foot-tunnel exit **AD**, with your back to the river, go anticlockwise (to your right) around the Waterfront Leisure Centre. Or go clockwise to pass toilets. At A206 Woolwich High Street **AE**, cross at the traffic lights and keep ahead along Hare Street, where you pass bus stops. Turn left at the end along the semi-pedestrianised Powis Street **AF**. At the end is Beresford Square, with toilets adjacent to Beresford Gate to your left. Turn right along Greens End **AG**, then left beside General Gordon Place, where there are more bus stops. The entrance to Woolwich Arsenal Station **AH** lies ahead across New Road.*

# USEFUL
# INFORMATION

# Transport

It will make good sense for most Capital Ring walkers to use public transport. This offers many advantages, even for regular motorists. For a start, parking for long periods is difficult or impractical in many areas. You won't need to get back to your car, which may not be easy when the finish of the walk is several miles from the start. It also means you can forget about the security of your vehicle, minimise pollution and have a beer or two with no qualms. Travelcards or pensioners' Freedom Cards are likely to provide best value for getting to the route: all of the Capital Ring lies within Zones 2, 3 and 4. More information follows, but remember that it is subject to change — always check with the relevant travel information line.

### Travelcards and Bus Passes

The one-day off-peak Travelcard gives great freedom of movement, allowing you to change from train to tube to bus to tram at will within Greater London. It is valid after 9.30 a.m. Monday to Friday, and any time at weekends or on public holidays. At a higher cost, the peak Travelcard will give you the same freedom before 9.30 a.m. For adults, the cost varies according to the number of zones you want to travel through, but there is a flat rate for children aged five to 15. There are several other kinds of Travelcard, for example a Weekend Travelcard will save you 25 per cent on the cost of two separate cards for Saturday and Sunday. It can also be used on two consecutive days of a public-holiday weekend. A Family Travelcard offers a saving on individual Travelcards when one or two adults are travelling with up to four children, with a very low flat rate for the children. They need not be related, but must travel together.

You can buy Travelcards at tube stations, most London railway stations, London Transport Information Centres, and at over 2300 pass agents around London — usually local newsagents displaying the 'Pass Agent' sign. There are six zones in total, and when you buy your card you must state which zones you intend to travel through. The more zones, the higher the fare, with Zone 1 (Central London) being the most expensive. Remember that even if the start and finish of your walk are in outer zones, your Travelcard must cover the inner zones if you need to travel through them to or from your destination.

If you intend to travel by bus for all your journeys, Bus Passes are much cheaper. The bus network is divided into four zones. Zones 1, 2 and 3 are approximately the same as the Travelcard zones, but Zone 4 covers Travelcard Zones 4, 5 and 6. In addition, all Travelcards are valid over the corresponding bus network.

## Travel Information

Most transport services in Zones 2, 3 and 4 are reasonably frequent, even on Saturdays and Sundays. However, some services operate less frequently at weekends and in a few cases not at all on Sundays. You are advised to check service details in advance: for London tube and bus services, tel: 020 7222 1234, for National Rail Enquiries, tel: 08457 484950 — both lines are open 24 hours a day. They should also be able to confirm which zones are included in your journeys. Information is also available at www.tfl.gov.uk.

## The starting points

These are the starting points, all at stations, for each of the 15 walks of the Capital Ring. Each has a frequent service from Central London, usually at least every 30 minutes. There are other options where you can start or finish: at stations, as shown, plus many points in between served by buses. This information is only intended as a guide, and you should check it by calling the travel information services mentioned above.

*Walk Zone*

| | | |
|---|---|---|
| 1 | 4 | **Woolwich Arsenal** (for Foot Tunnel). Connex from Charing Cross, Waterloo East, London Bridge or Cannon Street. Other station with Capital Ring link: Woolwich Dockyard. Riverbus: Thames Barrier. |
| 2 | 4 | **Falconwood**. Connex from Charing Cross, Waterloo East, London Bridge, Cannon Street or Victoria. Other station with Capital Ring link: Mottingham. |
| 3 | 4 | **Grove Park**. Connex from Charing Cross, Waterloo East, London Bridge or Cannon Street. Other station passed: Penge East. Other stations with Capital Ring link: Ravensbourne, Kent House, Penge West. |
| 4 | 4 | **Crystal Palace**. South Central from London Bridge or Victoria. Other station with Capital Ring link: Streatham. |
| 5 | 3 | **Streatham Common**. South Central from Victoria. Other stations passed: Wandsworth Common, Earlsfield. Other station with Capital Ring link: Balham. |
| 6 | 3 | **Wimbledon Park**. District Line from Central London. |
| 7 | 4 | **Richmond**. District Line from London. South West Trains from Waterloo. Silverlink Trains North London Line. Other station with Capital Ring link: Brentford. |
| 8 | 4 | **Boston Manor** (for Osterley Lock). Piccadilly Line from Central London. Other station passed: South Greenford. Other station with Capital Ring link: Hanwell. |

| | | |
|---|---|---|
| 9 | 4 | **Greenford**. Central Line from Central London. Thames Trains from Paddington. Other stations passed: Sudbury Hill, Sudbury Hill Harrow. Other stations with Capital Ring link: Harrow-on-the-Hill, Northwick Park. |
| 10 | 4 | **South Kenton**. Bakerloo Line from Central London. Silverlink Trains from Euston. Other stations passed: Preston Road. Other stations with Capital Ring link: Wembley Park, Hendon. |
| 11 | 3/4 | **Hendon Central** (for Hendon Park). Northern Line from Central London. Other station passed: East Finchley. Note that Hendon Central is in Zone 3 if you are travelling from Zones 1, 2 or 3, but in Zone 4 if travelling from Zones 4, 5 or 6, or from outside Greater London. |
| 12 | 3 | **Highgate**. Northern Line from Central London. Other station passed: Manor House. Other stations with Capital Ring link: Crouch Hill, Finsbury Park. |
| 13 | 2 | **Stoke Newington**. WAGN from Liverpool Street. Other station with Capital Ring link: Clapton. |
| 14 | 2 | **Hackney Wick**. Silverlink Trains North London Line (change at Stratford or Highbury & Islington for Central London). Other stations with Capital Ring link: Pudding Mill Lane, West Ham. |
| 15 | 3 | **Royal Albert** (for Beckton District Park). Docklands Light Railway from Bank. Other stations passed: Cyprus, Gallions Reach, North Woolwich. Other station with Capital Ring link: Woolwich Arsenal. |

# USEFUL ADDRESSES

**British Walking Federation**, 112 Crescent Road, Reading RG1 5SW. E-mail: info@bwf-ivv.org.uk. Net: www.bwf-ivv.org.uk *Through its member clubs, organises non-competitive events and permanent trails for people of all ages and abilities, who receive awards for their achievement.*

**British Waterways**, Willow Grange, Church Road, Watford WD17 4QA. Tel: 01923 201120. Fax: 01923 201400. E-mail: enquiries.hq@britishwaterways.co.uk. Net: www.britishwaterways.co.uk *Manages and cares for 2000 miles of canals, navigable rivers and docks, including the Grand Union Canal and Lee Navigation.*

**Corporation of London**, Guildhall, PO Box 270, London EC2P 2EJ. Tel: 020 7606 3030. Fax: 020 7332 1119. E-mail: pro@corpoflondon.gov.uk

Net: www.corpoflondon.gov.uk *Owns and manages many open spaces in and near London, including Highgate Wood.*
**English Heritage**, PO Box 569, Swindon SN2 2YP.
Tel: 0870 333 1181. Fax: 01793 414926. E-mail: customers@ english-heritage.org.uk. Net: www.english-heritage.org.uk *Maintains many historic properties including Eltham Palace.*
**Greater London Authority**, City Hall, The Queen's Walk, Southwark, London SE1 2AA. Tel: 020 7983 4000. Fax: 020 7983 4057. E-mail: mayor@london.gov.uk. Net: www.london.gov.uk
**Lee Valley Park**, Information Centre, Abbey Gardens, Waltham Abbey EN9 1XQ. Tel: 01992 702200. Fax: 01992 702230.
E-mail: info@leevalleypark.org.uk. Net: www.leevalleypark.com
**Living Streets**, 31 Bondway, Vauxhall, London SW8 1SJ.
Tel: 020 7820 1010. Fax: 020 7820 8208. E-mail: info@livingstreets.org.uk.
Net: www.livingstreets.org.uk *Formerly the Pedestrians Association, campaigns for better and safer conditions for all pedestrians.*
**London Boroughs**. *Responsible for highway and footpath maintenance, and for management of most of the parks along the Capital Ring. Their parks departments can provide details of park closing times, where relevant.*
**Barnet**. Town Hall, The Burroughs, Hendon, London NW4 4BG.
Tel: 020 8359 4000. Fax: 020 8359 2197.
E-mail: info.centre@barnet.gov.uk. Net: www.barnet.gov.uk
**Brent**. Town Hall, Forty Lane, Wembley, Middlesex HA9 9HD.
Tel: 020 8937 1234. Fax: 020 8937 1202. E-mail:
customer.services@brent.gov.uk. Net: www.brent.gov.uk
**Bromley**. Civic Centre, Stockwell Close, Bromley, Kent BR1 3UH.
Tel: 020 8464 3333. E-mail: signpost@bromley.gov.uk
Net: www.bromley.gov.uk
**Croydon**. Council Offices, Taberner House, Park Lane, Croydon CR9 3JS. Tel: 020 8686 4433. Fax: 020 8760 0871.
E-mail: corp_info@croydon.gov.uk. Net: www.croydon.gov.uk
**Ealing**. Council Offices, Perceval House, 14 Uxbridge Road, Ealing, London W5 2HL. Tel: 020 8825 5000. E-mail:
customers@ealing.gov.uk. Net: www.ealing.gov.uk
**Greenwich**. Town Hall, Wellington Street, Woolwich, London SE18 6PM. Tel: 020 8854 8888. E-mail: via website.
Net: www.greenwich.gov.uk
**Hackney**. Town Hall, Mare Street, Hackney, London E8 1EA. Tel: 020 8356 5000. E-mail: fss@hackney.gov.uk. Net: www.hackney.gov.uk
**Haringey**. Civic Centre, High Road, Wood Green, London N22 8LE.
Tel: 020 8489 0000. E-mail: webcoordinator@haringey.gov.uk
Net: www.haringey.gov.uk

**Harrow**. Civic Centre, Station Road, Harrow, Middlesex HA1 2UU. Tel: 020 8863 5611. Fax: 020 8424 1134. E-mail: info@harrow.gov.uk. Net: www.harrow.gov.uk

**Hounslow**. Civic Centre, Lampton Road, Hounslow, Middlesex TW3 4DN. Tel: 020 8583 2000. Fax: 020 8583 2598. E-mail: via website. Net: www.hounslow.gov.uk

**Islington**. Town Hall, Upper Street, Islington, London N1 2UD. Tel: 020 7527 2000. E-mail: via website. Net: www.islington.gov.uk

**Kingston-upon-Thames** (Royal Borough of). Guildhall, High Street, Kingston, Surrey KT1 1EU. Tel: 020 8546 2121. E-mail: via website. Net: www.kingston.gov.uk

**Lambeth**. Town Hall, Brixton Hill, Brixton, London SW2 1RW. Tel: 020 7926 1000. E-mail: infodesk@lambeth.gov.uk. Net: www.lambeth.gov.uk

**Lewisham**. Town Hall, Catford Road, Catford, London SE6 4RU. Tel: 020 8314 6000. E-mail: via website. Net: www.lewisham.gov.uk

**Merton**. Civic Centre, London Road, Morden, Surrey SM4 5DX. Tel: 020 8543 2222. E-mail: postroom@merton.gov.uk. Net: www.merton.gov.uk

**Newham**. Town Hall, Barking Road, East Ham, London E6 2RP. Tel: 020 8430 2000. E-mail: customer.services@newham.gov.uk. Net: www.newham.gov.uk

**Richmond-upon-Thames**. Civic Centre, 44 York Street, Twickenham, Middlesex TW1 3BZ. Tel: 020 8891 1411. E-mail: web.team@richmond.gov.uk. Net: www.richmond.gov.uk

**Tower Hamlets**. Town Hall, Mulberry Place, 5 Clove Crescent, Blackwall, London E14 2BG. Tel: 020 7364 5000. Fax: 020 7364 3063. E-mail: webteam@towerhamlets.gov.uk Net: www.towerhamlets.gov.uk

**Waltham Forest**. Town Hall, Forest Road, Walthamstow, London E17 4JF. Tel: 020 8527 5544. Fax: 020 8527 8313. E-mail: wfdirect@lbwf.gov.uk. Net: www.lbwf.gov.uk

**Wandsworth**. Town Hall, Wandsworth High Street, London SW18 2PU. Tel: 020 8871 6000. Fax: 020 8871 7560. E-mail: via website. Net: www.wandsworth.gov.uk

**London Wildlife Trust**, Harling House, 47 Great Suffolk Street, London SE1 0BS. Tel: 020 7261 0447. Fax: 020 7261 0538. E-mail: enquiries@wildlondon.org.uk. Net: www.wildlondon.org.uk
*Cares for over 50 nature reserves in Greater London, including several along the Capital Ring.*

**Long Distance Walkers Association**, c/o 63 Yockley Close, Camberley, Surrey GU15 1QQ. E-mail: membership@ldwa.org.uk. Net: www.ldwa.org.uk

*Represents interests of long distance walkers and organises walks through a network of groups, including one for London.*
**Open Spaces Society**, 25a Bell Street, Henley-on-Thames, Berkshire RG9 2BA. Tel: 01491 573535. Fax: 01491 573051. E-mail: hq@oss.org.uk. Net: www.oss.org.uk
*Protects common land, greens and open spaces.*
**Ordnance Survey**, Romsey Road, Southampton S016 4GU. Tel: 08456 050505. Fax: 023 8079 2615.
E-mail: enquiries@ordsvy.gov.uk. Net: www.ordsvy.gov.uk
*Publishes maps covering the whole of the United Kingdom.*
**Ramblers' Association**, 2nd Floor, Camelford House, 87 Albert Embankment, Vauxhall, London SE1 7TW. Tel: 020 7339 8500. Fax: 020 7339 8501. E-mail: ramblers@london.ramblers.org.uk Net: www.ramblers.org.uk
*Takes up path problems and organises walks through a network of local groups, including 20 covering Greater London.*
**TfL Street Management**, Walking Promotions Office, 25 Eccleston Place, London SW1W 9NF. E-mail: walking@tfl.gov.uk
Net: www.tfl.gov.uk/walking
**Thames River Services**, Westminster Pier, Victoria Embankment, London SW1A 2JH. Tel: 020 7930 4097. Fax: 020 7930 1616.
E-mail: boats@westminsterpier.co.uk. Net: www.westminsterpier.co.uk
**Tourist Information Centres** *can offer help with local accommodation, transport and details of places to visit:*
**Central London**. Glen House, Stag Place, Victoria, London SW1E 5LT. Tel: 020 7932 2000. Fax: 020 7932 0222.
E-mail: enquiries@londontouristboard.co.uk
Net: www.londontouristboard.co.uk
**Croydon**. Croydon Clocktower, Katharine Street, Croydon CR9 1ET. Tel: 020 8253 1009. Fax: 020 8253 1008.
E-mail: tic@croydononline.org
**Harrow**. Civic Centre, Station Road, Harrow, Middlesex HA1 2XF. Tel: 020 8424 1102. Fax: 020 8424 1134.
E-mail: info@harrow.gov.uk
**Hounslow**. The Treaty Centre, High Street, Hounslow, Middlesex TW3 1ES. Tel: 0845 4562929. Fax: 0845 456 2904.
E-mail: tic@hounslow.gov.uk
**Kingston**. Market House, Market Place, Kingston, Surrey KT1 1JS. Tel: 020 8547 5592. Fax: 020 8547 5594.
**Richmond**. Old Town Hall, Whittaker Avenue, Richmond, Surrey TW9 1TP. Tel: 020 8940 9125. Fax: 020 8940 6899.
E-mail: information.services@richmond.gov.uk

# Ordnance Survey Maps Covering The Capital Ring

**Landranger Maps** (scale 1:50 000): 176 West London area and 177 East London area.

**Explorer Maps** (scale 1:25 000): 162 Greenwich & Gravesend, 161 London South, 173 London North. Parts of Walks 12 and 13 also appear on 174 Epping Forest & Lea Valley, but this duplicates the sections included on sheet 162.